The Cure

FOR GROUPS

How to Lead a Small Group People Will Talk
About the Rest of Their Lives

ROBBY ANGLE

PRAISE FOR

The Cure for Groups

"It doesn't matter whether you're a virtual group, an in-person group, a book club, a university campus group, a monthly business group, or a church group, this much-needed book will help you thrive."

—*Tom Shefchunas, Executive Director of Youth Specialties*

"This is the book every small group leader should read and embody. Angle guides you through creating a community that is intentional, authentic, and life-changing."

—*Clay Scroggins, Lead Pastor Buckhead Church and Author of*
How to Lead When You're Not in Charge

"A practical and timely resource for any small group leader."

—*Brad Lomenick, Author and Founder of BLINC*

"In *The Cure for Groups*, Robby Angle lays out a clear process for thriving small groups. His practical tips are invaluable, and they are found throughout the book. But, there is more to this than just an excellent small group experience. Robby is really 'angling' for Christians to develop the type of high-trust grace-filled relationships that Trueface has been encouraging for decades. Your life and relationships will be enriched by spending time with *The Cure for Groups*."

—*David H. Wills, President Emeritus,*
National Christian Foundationl

"Angle provides practical tools to enable genuine community and relationships that lead to hope, health and joy. *The Cure for Groups* is an incredible resource for anyone seeking to grow such a community."

—*Lindy Black, Associate U. S. Director, The Navigators*

"Ever since the first Twelve, many Jesus-followers have found group experiences to be transformative. Good groups, that is. *The Cure for Groups* offers insight and practical help to make group life a great environment to support a people-development culture. Thanks, Robby, for sharing your obvious and considerable expertise!"

—*Reggie McNeal, Senior Fellow, Leadership Network*

"In *The Cure for Groups* Robby pulls back the curtain on why so many spiritual growth groups flounder, then he shows us a door we can enter where groups—made up of authentic relationships—are life altering and life giving. I wish this book were around when I was training seminary students."

—*Michael John Cusick, CEO at Restoring the Soul & Author of* Surfing for God

"On this side of Heaven, deep and healthy relationships with other people can be so hard. *The Cure for Groups* is one of the best relational and practical tools I have seen for the process of growing closer to God and people in the context of community."

— *Franni Rae Cash Cain, Singer/Songwriter, We The Kingdom*

"This is such a practical and insightful book for anyone leading a small group. This is like the GPS navigation that we all need as small group leaders."

—*Brian Mosley, President, RightNow Media*

"In *The Cure for Groups*, you will find the master plan for leading small groups that are certain to transform participants, their families and the communities where they live. Discover how to effectively cultivate life-long relationships and eternal life change!"

—*Tami Heim, President & CEO, Christian Leadership Alliance*

"In our two decades of leadership, counseling and executive coaching, we know people are starving for more than content-driven resources and feel uncertain where to turn. Robby Angle has created an accessible "how-to" guide for any small group, providing a roadmap to transformational relationships that are both rooted in grace and meet the deeper needs people are longing for today."

—*Jeff & Terra Mattson,* Authors of Shrinking the Integrity Gap: Between What Leaders Preach & Live *and* Courageous *and Co-Founders of Living Wholehearted and Courageous Girls.*

"Some books can be skimmed, but some books need to be read slowly and reflected on deeply. What Robby Angle has provided us in *The Cure for Groups* is the latter. Not because it's not easily accessible in how it's written, but because the concepts presented are spot on for anyone wanting to lead a group that people will talk about for a long, long time. Read it, reflect on it, but most importantly, be sure to apply it in your life and group leadership."

—*Bill Willits,* Executive Director of Adult Ministries at North Point Ministries, Co-Author of Creating Community

"Have you ever experienced true acceptance? A place where you have the freedom to live out your God-given design? A place where you aren't compelled to perform? A place where people truly accept you? These are "Environments of Grace!" Speaking from personal experience I have experienced the principles Robby Angle outlines in *The Cure for Groups,* they work! So come, join the journey with us. Recruit others to experience grace with you . . . and be all you were created to be!"

—*Lauren Libby,* International President/CEO, TWR International

Dedication

For my number one small group.

I love you, Emily. You are the most loving and wise woman I know. It is a blast co-leading our group of eight amazing kids—Moses, Zane, Naomi, Jude, Titus, Valor, Emmie, and Eli. Even though ten people are probably more than I would recommend for an ideal small group size, it is perfect for us.

Contents

Setting Sail

"If you want to build a ship, don't drum up the men and women to gather wood, divide the work, and give orders. Instead, teach them to yearn for the vast and endless sea."

—ANTOINE DE SAINT-EXUPERY

"I just," she paused for a moment. "I don't want to be in another boring group."

She being Leslie. You'll meet her in a few pages. Let's face it though, a lot of us have been there, right? We may not have said it out loud, but we've felt it. Too many small groups sadly come up short. They're, well, kinda lame. You go and exchange small talk with people you've been meeting with for months but still barely know. They ask you about information they memorized from the week before, saying, "Hey, you said last week you had a big meeting. How'd that go?" You reply, "Oh, it went well. Thanks for asking." Then, after an awkward silence, you make an excuse to go get some more chips and dip.

What comes next is even more draining. You go through some kind of scripture or curriculum, and everyone gives the "right" answers. If someone does share something real, no one's really sure what to do. You might want to move closer or offer some comfort, but, well, you're not *close* enough for that. You end with prayer requests that feel sterile and safe, and you all thank whoever brought the snacks.

On your drive home you find yourself wondering if your time would have been better spent taking care of a few errands or just getting dinner with some friends who actually know you. That voice in your head is loud. *What is even the point of this? I thought I'd finally make some really good friends and grow more in my faith. Instead, I just feel lonelier and like I'm checking a spiritual box. Nothing's changing. What's wrong?*

It's boring the life out of you. That's what's wrong.

This is the kind of group people dread going to, and it's the kind of group a leader dreads leading.

It doesn't have to be this way. In fact, it *shouldn't* be this way.

There are groups out there that are deep, real, challenging, and a blast to be a part of—where people are their authentic, unfiltered selves, where they laugh a lot and are the first to show up when someone's in crisis, where they are willing to challenge each other because they really know and love each other, and where their relationships lead to genuine life change.

You can be a part of that kind of group. You can lead that kind of group. This book will show you how.

• • •

You Were Made for This

The desire to be fully known and loved is in our bones. God designed us to grow spiritually by connecting relationally. This truth will never change, no matter how digitally connected we become. In their research at Barna Group, David Kinnaman and Mark Matlock found that among "resilient disciples" who are between 18 and 29 years old, 85% have someone in their life who encourages them to grow spiritually, and 82% are connected to a community of Christians.[1] Put another way, real, authentic relationships are vital to our spiritual growth. We innately have a deep longing for these kinds of relationships, to live in that space beyond the mask where our shame and insecurities fall away and we are able to experience the freedom, peace, and joy of deep, meaningful relationships with others. We were made for it.

God is relational to the core. We see it first in the Trinity, how the Father, Son, and Holy Spirit live in perfect relationship with each other. We see it in God's declaration that it is not good for man to be alone. We see this relational imperative throughout the stories of the Bible as David relies on wisdom from Jonathan, Ruth meets God through her relationship with Naomi, and Daniel, Shadrach, Meshach, and Abednego navigate the temptations and persecution of Babylon together. Most powerfully, we see it in the life of Jesus of Nazareth. Somehow this obscure carpenter's son and his ragtag group of disciples from an insignificant outpost on the fringe of the Roman Empire turned Western civilization upside

GOD CHOSE TO CHANGE THE WORLD THROUGH A SMALL GROUP OF PEOPLE CONNECTING DEEPLY WITH GOD AND EACH OTHER.

down, and they did it through their relationships. Jesus's countercultural, counterintuitive teachings redefined our relationship with God and our relationships with others.

God chose to change the world through a small group of people connecting deeply with God and each other. They learned who God is and who he said they were, and they lived out a transformational reality that was undeniable and contagious.

5

Jesus modeled for us a relational ministry. He designed his church—his *ecclesia*, or gathering of believers—to continue along these lines. He still changes the world that way.

So, Why Isn't It Working?

If we are made for these kinds of life-altering relationships, and if Jesus modeled them for us, then why do so many of us drag our feet going to our small group? Why do many groups feel forced, fake, and stagnant? Why does it feel like something we're checking off the list and isn't leading to the kind of relationships and spiritual growth we hoped for?

The simple answer is this: we're afraid.

Fear is one of the strongest and most difficult emotions to control. This book will help you learn more about how to nurture, tend, and care for fear's opposite, more powerful emotion in relationships: love.[2]

There are three levels that describe our relationships. And most of us get dead scared around level two and rarely experience the love, freedom, and growth that accompanies level three relationships. Level three is where the gold is. It is where we experience deep connections that are critical in helping us mature in our relationship with God.

Three Levels of Relationships

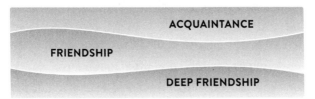

LEVEL ONE

This is the acquaintance level. We make social connections with people who enjoy the same things as us, the same hobbies or interests. Maybe our kids play together. We may be on the same project at work or in the same running club. These relationships are convenient and meet a need we have. We share surface level things, just small nuggets of truth about ourselves, and with enough time, these small nuggets slowly build up, creating little blocks of trust that can eventually lead to level two. Perfect love *does* cast out fear—but only if you trust it.

LEVEL TWO

This is the friendship level. As friends, we invite each other to come closer to see a little more of us. We hang out in this space for a while because there are lots of safe things to share and to trust others with. Level two is a great stage where we each benefit from and enjoy the relationship. However, at the core, friendships are still primarily about us. This smaller group of our friends help us have fun, feel loved, and feel connected. Most of us experience this level of relationship and rarely venture past it.

We get stuck here because we're afraid.

There's a tension between the second and third levels called shame. Shame whispers to us, telling us that this person is our friend *now* while they know the easier, safer parts of us, but if we let them into the darker rooms of our hearts, then they'll reject us.

So, we stay at level two, hiding the things we're ashamed of and wondering why we still don't feel that deep connection we long for. We trust more than we did at level one, but there are still a lot of caveats. Level two is just too comfortable to leave, but when we stay there, we miss out on what level three has to offer—and what we really desire.

LEVEL THREE

This is the level of deep friendship. It's a place where the best and worst of you can be known by the other person. It's a place where the other person knows your ugly stories and doesn't move an inch. It's a place where you don't have any more, "Well, I don't know if they'd accept me if they knew *that*." Level three relationships are where you feel fully known and fully loved, where love truly casts out fear because you've trusted the other person.

Level three relationships are more about the other person than about us. It is where we protect each other's weaknesses and submit to each other's strengths, being healthier and stronger through those relationships than we are without them. These relationships are consistent and intentional. A level three relationship usually takes time to develop and a conversation to speak to the importance and priority of the relationship. It is in this rare space that a level three friend would know that I have not been prioritizing time with my wife in a busy work season, and he would ask me about it because he loves me and wants better for me.

So, what does this have to do with groups? I want to be clear: *relationships* are central to our spiritual growth, not groups. God has designed us to grow through community with other Jesus followers. In a busy world where life-changing relationships are hard to come by, groups can help us find and develop those relationships.

RELATIONSHIPS ARE CENTRAL TO OUR SPIRITUAL GROWTH, NOT GROUPS.

Groups provide a structure for us to have more consistent and intentional time with others, which therefore helps us develop deeper relationships. Those relationships lead to authentic community, which becomes an environment for spiritual growth as we mature and grow together. Another benefit of groups is that they help us grow in unique ways as we experience living in grace within a large, complex community.

One of the reasons I am passionate about helping people develop amazing small groups is because they have been the primary place to help me find level two relationships over the past twenty years. Those level two relationships have then developed into level three relationships where I feel fully known and fully loved. Those relationships have changed my life and have had an incredible impact on my faith journey.

Now, some of you might be thinking, "That all sounds great, but how do I actually *do* this stuff?"

You know, I was hoping you'd ask that.

Hi. I'm Robby. I'm Here to Help.

I've been fascinated by groups for a long time. Earlier in my professional career I was a Licensed Professional Counselor in Boone, NC, leading group therapy sessions. I then went to North Point Community Church in Alpharetta, GA—one of the largest churches in the country—where I got to reimagine an approach to groups.

To be honest, I started to nerd out on this whole idea of groups. I'm an analytical guy and wanted to know if getting together with a group of people consistently and intentionally actually leads to spiritual growth. My position at North Point provided an amazing opportunity to carefully and methodically study hundreds of groups, discovering the principles and practices that separated the truly transformational groups from the average or below average ones. It's not often that you get to set up your own research and development lab to study real people in real groups, and I ran with it.

I gathered the wisest men and women I could find. I interviewed countless leaders and group members to discern which subtle—or not so subtle—differentiators led to life change, and which ones stifled it. I pored over dozens of models, books, and studies, I went to conferences, I consulted other thought leaders, and I led half a dozen different types of groups myself.

We stepped back from the "how" and started tinkering with the "why" behind amazing groups. We asked leaders what they actually needed and wanted. We identified the best leaders and tested best practices based on the principles we were discovering. There were five aspects that started coming out—five Core Components that seemed to consistently lead to transformational, talk about for the rest of your life kind of groups.

Clay Scroggins was my boss, group co-leader, and close friend during those eight years. He encouraged me to write this book, and I am incredibly thankful for his leadership. He asked me to figure out how to transfer these five Core Components into *all* of our adult groups at North Point so that transformational groups would be the norm instead of the exception. We started to see groups shift toward the kind of spiritual growth and connection we were hoping for all along.

I want to help you understand and apply those same principles in *your* group. I'll share the five Core Components that build transformational groups and equip you to lead the kind of group people talk about for the rest of their lives (in a good way). These five Core Components can be applied in any group whose goal is to experience spiritual growth, whether in the business, organizational, church, or academic sphere. Together, they will help you avoid boring, stagnant groups and replace them with healthy, enjoyable, life-transforming groups.

• • •

The Five Core Components

We'll unpack each of these Core Components through the next five chapters, both through teaching and through getting to watch brand new leaders Stuart and Leslie navigate these principles in their group.

To help you remember these five Core Components, we've put them into a metaphor of going on a sailing voyage. The five

Components correspond to five aspects of setting sail that are vital for a successful adventure:

 The Destination:
Determine the Goals of Your Group

 The Captain:
Lead with Intentionality and Vulnerability

 The Crew:
Clarify Your Group Culture

 The Ship:
Design Your Time for Transformation

 The Route:
Plan Ahead to Get Where You Want to Go

These five Core Components differentiate exceptional leaders and transformational groups from typical or boring ones. They will provide you with a framework to build a Group Map to help get you where you want to go. With that said, none of these in and of themselves are a silver bullet. Ultimately, the Holy Spirit guides our relationships, and even the most well-prepared groups sometimes just don't take off. However, from my years of studying which groups become *that* group, I have found that these five aspects are the most pivotal and powerful to building a truly transformational group.

What This Book Is and Isn't

So, do these five Components *cure* lame small groups? Not necessarily. But they can help.

The health and maturity of the leader is the greatest determinant of the efficacy of any small group, just like in other teams, businesses, ministries, and organizations. The foundation of any leader is found in their view of God—their theology—and their view of themselves— their identity.

I believe the health and maturity of the leader makes up about 60% of the small group equation. The best teaching I have found that addresses the theology and identity that shapes the core of the leader is already written about in the book *The Cure*, by John Lynch, Bruce McNicol, and Bill Thrall.[3] This book has helped me—along with hundreds of thousands of others— mature into who Jesus made me to be as a new creation. It has had a huge impact on my life, and I strongly recommend it as a key resource for any leader or group.

> I BELIEVE THE HEALTH AND MATURITY OF THE LEADER MAKES UP ABOUT 60% OF THE SMALL GROUP EQUATION.

If 60% of the small group equation is the health of the leader, I would say 25% is determined by the best practices of that leader in facilitating a group, with the remaining 15% made up by group variables like chemistry, life events, and other dynamics that you have little control over. While we will venture into a higher-level discussion on how a leader views God and themselves and how that affects their group, the majority of this book will focus on equipping you with some best practices, the 25%. These are the practical, how-to tools for a group.

Small groups are a key discipleship tool for most churches and faith-based organizations, but practical best practices are hard to find. These five Core Components work to help direct a new group or re-focus an existing group. They will serve virtual groups, in-person groups, or hybrid groups. They will help redirect lame groups and refine already great groups. They will further develop the new leader, the group member, or the seasoned leader.

Don't be overwhelmed. You are right where you should be on your journey. Every day each of us gets a fresh opportunity to trust God and others with ourselves, maturing into who we already are as forgiven and righteous sons and daughters.[4] Leading groups is difficult and not for the faint of heart, but it's worth it. You won't use everything recommended in this book, but our hope is that you will be equipped to lead more effectively. The Father designed us for connecting relationally to grow spiritually, Jesus made it possible, and the Holy Spirit will guide us. Enjoy the journey.

Leader Resources

At *trueface.org/cureforgroups*, you'll find a one-page **Group Map** for you to download. Use this as you navigate through the Core Components with your group, recording your destination, crew culture, and more. This will keep everything in one place and provide an easy way to refer back to what you've decided as a group.

The five Core Components taught in this book are best accompanied and implemented with our small group guide *Embark: A Six-Part Study to Launch Your Group*. *Embark* guides your small group through each of the Core Components, laying a foundation for the kind of group you'll talk about for the rest of your life. *The Cure for Groups* is for you, the leader. *Embark* is for your group as you move through these five Components. Learn more at *www.trueface.org*.

The Destination

DETERMINE THE GOALS OF YOUR GROUP

"If one does not know to which port one is sailing, no wind is favorable."

—LUCIUS ANNAEUS SENECA

Before you get on a ship—unless you're trying to skip town with a bunch of gold—you need to know where it's going and whether you're willing to commit to the journey. Voyages are long. You don't want to embark on that kind of journey without knowing what the destination is. As Yogi Berra put it, "If you don't know where you're going, you'll end up someplace else."

Just like sailing a successful voyage, this question of destination is foundational for any group that wants to grow together. Where do you want to go? Why are you going on this journey? Does everyone agree on the same destination, or are you all trying to get somewhere different? Deciding ahead of time on your destination will save a lot of unnecessary conflict and unmet expectations.

Up ahead we get a bird's eye view as Stuart and Leslie, our brand new small group leaders, begin their maiden voyage of leading a group. Their journey will help us see the five Core Components tried out in a real group—sometimes in smooth seas and sometimes in rough waters.

• • •

Stuart and Leslie's Kitchen, Thursday Night, 6:15 p.m.

Leslie couldn't help herself from looking out the window every few minutes. "Do you think they'll be on time?"

Her husband, Stuart, looked over from the kitchen. "What? I couldn't hear you over the ice machine." He jangled a cup of ice as proof.

"Nothing," she murmured. They had enough snacks and drinks to supply a doomsday bunker. Their kiddos were at her mom's. Leslie had arranged the living room with as many seats as possible. She kept wondering if she had forgotten something.

"Les, it's going to be fine," Stuart called from the kitchen. "People don't expect that much the first night."

Leslie sighed and turned away from the window. She believed people *did* expect a lot from the first night. First impressions are important. She tried to let that thought go as she walked back in the kitchen, leaning her elbows on the island. "Alright. I'm really glad we talked to Tim and Jane first. That helped. But . . . I just . . . ," she paused for a moment, and Stuart raised his eyebrows in question. "I don't want to be in another boring group. I definitely don't want to *lead* a boring group."

Stuart laughed. He loved Leslie's honesty. He squeezed her shoulders and said, "Me neither. It's going to be great. I've got the flipcharts all ready."

She rolled her eyes and muttered, "Right, because that makes me feel better." The doorbell rang, and her stomach clenched.

People trickled in over the next fifteen minutes. First was Erik, who had been a friend of Stuart's for a few years—mid-thirties, professional, divorced. He never talked much about his story, though Leslie had often wondered.

Amy showed up next. She was in her late twenties and worked at the nearby university. Leslie had always thought she seemed nice but had really struggled to connect with her. She was always, "Fine!" or "Good!" or "Blessed!"

Next came Melissa, practically dragging Mike. Mike grunted, "Hello," and made a beeline for the beverage table. Melissa, on the other hand, lingered in the entryway talking at warp speed, complimenting everything she saw. Stuart and Leslie realized right away that Mike's presence was forced. They glanced at each other and read the other's mind. "Now this should be fun."

Then Leslie heard voices she knew, and Dwayne and Keisha walked in the front door. Close friends of her and Stuart for the last few years, their arrival instantly calmed her nerves. She trusted Keisha and Dwayne. "We can do this," she reminded herself as everyone grouped around the snacks and exchanged small talk.

It was only a few weeks ago that Stuart and Leslie had offered to lead a small group, feeling like it was time for them to take a more active role in their church. "Skin in the game," Leslie called it. They had been assigned this new group, and after a half-day training, they found themselves with people in their home and only a vague idea of what to do.

About ten years ago, when Stuart and Leslie were first married, they had been part of another group. Stuart had met Tim through a mutual friend, and Tim had invited them to join a group of young married couples that he and his wife Jane were starting. In their forties at the time, Tim and Jane created an atmosphere for those young couples that made a huge impact on both Stuart and Leslie. It had been raw and real, and they saw actual changes in their own lives.

But that was ten years ago, and they hadn't experienced a group like that since. The groups that followed had all been . . . well, lackluster. Leslie, always honest, just called them "all hat, no cattle." She looked around the room as everyone stood eating chips and salsa. *God, please let this not suck.*

"Alright, we're moving to the living room. Claim your seat!" Stuart called, clapping his hands together. Leslie gave him a tentative smile. An extrovert to his core, these situations didn't seem to make him nearly as uncomfortable as they made Leslie.

Once everyone settled into the living room, Stuart asked them to go around and say their name, what they did for work, and where they grew up. He felt it was a good way to ease into this new group. He asked Leslie to start things off.

"Hi, I'm Leslie. I'm a veterinarian, and I grew up in Austin, Texas." Then it went around the room and everyone shared, even Mike. Things eventually made their way back to Stuart.

"Thanks, everybody. I'm Stuart. I teach history at the community college, and I grew up on the outskirts of Chicago. A few years ago Les and I were in a really awesome group that we loved, and there were a few things that we did differently in that group than in any group we've been a part of since. We thought we'd try some of those things out. I have been in some groups that, if I'm really honest, just didn't feel like they were worth my time," Stuart shrugged apologetically. "I don't want that to be the case for this group. I want to make sure whatever we do in this group ends up being worth our time."

Leslie smiled at him. "Now, I need to let y'all know that Stuart is really in love with flip charts. Like—I don't even understand how he finds this many opportunities to use them. I've seen him write our grocery list out on a flip chart, so just brace yourselves."

The group laughed a little as Stuart held up his hands and said, "And why was that weird?"

Leslie shook her head at him, then continued. "We called the couple that led that group Stuart mentioned and asked them for some pointers. One thing they strongly encouraged was to start by deciding what we want this group to be like. Or, I guess, why we want to do this group. All of us are here for different reasons, and each of us has different expectations. It seems wise to spend this first meeting just talking about expectations. So," she motioned to Stuart as he started peeling off flip chart sheets and sticking them to the wall, "here we go. Is it safe to assume we're all coming with some expectations for what this group will be like?"

Crickets. Nobody said a word. Melissa sort of nodded in agreement and Erik had that deer-in-headlights look. Leslie added, "I know, I know, that sounds corporate. Hang with us."

Stuart nodded and laughed as he turned to the three charts where he had written Relationship Expectations, Spiritual Growth Expectations, and Group Goals. He pointed to the first chart. "Okay, relationships. Let's talk up front about what we want and what we don't. I've tried to be a mind reader for years, and Leslie tells me I'm still bad at it, so we don't want to just guess at what you all want. We want to decide together."

"People are way more invested if they get to have a say in where you are leading them," Jane had told them over the phone. "If the group decides together where they want to go, they might stick around long enough to see if they get there."

"So, to start off, let's just brainstorm what we hope our relationships will look like in this group," Stuart continued. "How do we want this group to influence our relationships?"

More crickets.

At least Keisha and Dwayne looked thoughtful. Mike was staring off into space, clearly disengaged. Amy doodled in a notebook.

Leslie could actually hear the wall clock ticking from the kitchen. Or was that her heart beating?

Grief, somebody say something, Leslie thought desperately. She tried to look calm and patient, but it felt like the walls were closing in.

Finally, after another ten seconds of silence that felt like an hour, Keisha spoke up. "I would love for these relationships to feel real. My life is busy. I don't have time for fake stuff."

Everyone murmured agreement, and Leslie shot Keisha a grateful smile. Stuart wrote "real" on the sheet of paper.

"That's great. What else?" Leslie asked, hoping she sounded confident.

More silence. Even more fidgeting.

"Oh, crap!" Leslie suddenly stood up. "Wait, we're supposed to have sticky notes! This way, you can just write down ideas you have and then pass them all in. Sorry, I totally spaced that." She passed out the sticky notes and some pens and felt relieved as people started writing ideas down.

After a few minutes, Stuart collected all the notes, and then read them as he stuck them up on the sheet. "'Make new friends, learn from others, get more connected, have a good time, real relationships, have a group of people who know and understand me, improve my marriage, have fun.' This is a great list. Now, let's see if any of these can be grouped together."

They slowly combined a few of them and clarified others. Only Keisha, Erik, and Melissa were contributing. Or perhaps more accurately, Keisha and Erik were contributing, and Melissa was just flooding them with every thought and opinion that came to her. Everyone else stayed quiet, just nodding along.

"Alright, what's next Les?"

They repeated the sticky note approach with Spiritual Growth Expectations, and everyone took a few minutes to write out how they wanted to grow spiritually over the next year.

If Leslie thought Stuart was in his element, he wasn't. Internally, he felt like a rubber band stretched tight. He was trying to stay upbeat and positive, but getting the group to engage felt like pulling teeth. He was worried he'd run out of things to say any minute. And while he knew Leslie was nervous, he wished she'd speak up more to help him keep the ball rolling.

As they pared down the Spiritual Growth Expectations, Stuart thought he'd take a chance, trying to be brave and bold. That's what good leaders do, right?

"Mike, how do these sound to you?"

Mike stared at him blankly for a second, then shrugged. "Fine." Melissa rolled her eyes at her husband.

"Anything you would add?" Stuart tried to keep his voice casual, tamping down his discomfort.

"Nope," Mike replied, his tone clearly indicating he couldn't care less. Stuart wondered if Mike's honest answer would have been, "I don't want to be here, man."

"Great, what's next?" Stuart turned to Leslie, pretending his little bravery experiment wasn't a failure.

She took up the reins. "Okay, let's do another round of combining so we have a couple of group goals we can get behind. Let's try to land on a sentence or two for each of the relationship and spiritual expectations. This way we have something a little clearer."

Erik frowned. "So, what exactly would a relationship goal look like?"

"Well . . . ," Leslie started, trying to buy herself time. Her honest answer would have been "Beats me," but she felt like that wasn't a very leader-like thing to say. "You know, it could be something like, 'Our goal is to have real relationships where we live life together.'" She pointed to a couple of the categories of words on the flip chart as she said it.

Stuart nodded, impressed she'd come up with an example that easily. Leslie wondered if he knew she was faking it. "I like that, Les. What do you all think?"

They continued to awkwardly share and suggest, and after about ten minutes of discussion, Stuart stood up to read their two goal statements.

We want to have real relationships where we live life together and truly know and trust each other.

We want to help each other grow in love for God, self, and others.

"Alright, what do we think about that?" Stuart asked.

Everyone was nodding—well, everyone except Mike, but Stuart had decided to let Mike be Mike. Most people were actually smiling. Stuart felt a tiny bit of momentum. Maybe this exercise really was as helpful as Tim and Jane had said it would be.

Everyone was a little startled when Dwayne spoke up. "Honestly, if this group could actually become those two things, that would be amazing. I don't know how we get there, but let's give it a go. Even if we just got close, that'd be a big deal for me. I'm in."

Leslie agreed. "Me too. I want you all to know that I'm really going to prioritize this group. These goals feel important to me and Stuart. To tell you the truth, we have been in a

'YOU VALUE WHAT YOU PRIORITIZE, AND YOU PRIORITIZE WHAT YOU VALUE.'

season where we haven't felt connected to anyone really, and life has felt pretty flat. Work is crazy and the kids are crazier, and it just seems like these kinds of things have gotten squeezed out in all that mess."

Keisha responded, "Thanks, Les. It's like my old mentor used to say, 'You value what you prioritize, and you prioritize what you value.' I'm in too. I really want to put this group ahead of all the stuff that tries to keep me so busy and disconnected."

Leslie thought the walls felt a little farther away now. It was like there was air in the room and space for everyone, even Mike. She was thankful for Keisha. She was one of those women who didn't always speak up, but whenever she did, it was awesome.

Leslie glanced at Stuart as everyone started to gather their things. He smiled and said quietly, "First one down." Leslie nodded, taking a deep breath. *We can do this.*

First Meeting Tips

BUILD A COMFORTABLE ENVIRONMENT

- Check out *Embark* for some specific ideas, especially if you want to make the first meeting a social one.

- Starting with some fun questions, a cheesy icebreaker, or even just some good wings will help people loosen up a bit.

- Playing music at a low volume does wonders for making an environment feel more relaxed when people first arrive.

- Some groups will do a social to begin or jump right into curriculum depending on the circumstances. Trust your judgement as you know your unique group dynamics.

TACKLING LOGISTICS

- Sometime during the first night everyone needs to know the basic plan moving forward.

- Does everybody know where and when your next meeting is?

- Do you have their email addresses and phone numbers? Who is going to own the group communication?

What You Just Saw

The exercise we just saw Stuart and Leslie go through seems pretty simple and straightforward. But, why is it necessary? Why is determining your destination the first Core Component?

This Core Component actually applies beyond groups—it rests on the principle that knowing where you're going helps you get there. When God made us in his image,[5] He formed us with the capacity to determine goals that would help us get to better places in our journeys.

God has amazing plans for our lives, and understanding His intentions can

KNOWING WHERE YOU'RE GOING HELPS YOU GET THERE.

help provide direction for our journey, both as individuals and as a group.[6] Whether it's an education, a job we desire, or a family vacation, when we identify a destination we're much more likely to get there. If you don't clarify the destination as a group, then as the leader you're risking the valuable time each person invests in the group.

• • •

Why This Matters in Groups

Determining your destination as a group is vital to building a life-changing experience. When you embed this Core Component, you align your group expectations from the beginning, you protect everyone's time and emotional investment, and you lay the foundation for a group that loves being together and is committed to each other.

Clarifying your destination helps align people's expectations.
Your job as the captain of this metaphorical ship is to steer
the conversation and synthesize collective expectations. Do
you know why everyone is in the group and what they hope to
achieve by being involved? What are *your* expectations of the
group? Is your goal to make friends? To learn more about the
Bible? To experience an authentic community? To mature as
men or women? To improve your marriage? To fix your spouse?
(Hmm, you might want to reconsider that one). To mature in
your faith? To experience more of God's love? Many of us aren't
even aware of our expectations until they go unmet. Unmet
expectations are one of the most common sources of wounds
in relationships, so don't unnecessarily wound your group members. Most groups don't take time to clarify those expectations,
and then they wonder why people get frustrated.

*An hour of buy-in on the front end saves hours of realignment
on the back end.* When you ask your group to get involved,
you're inviting them to buy in from the beginning. You can be
certain they're asking themselves if this time investment is really
worth it. Think about your last ho-hum group. Didn't *you* have
your own set of hopes and expectations? So, if everyone has
their own idea of what the group experience should look like
and what they're hoping to accomplish, why not get that out
on the table from the get go? You're going to have to deal with
mismatches at some point. If you don't do this up front, you're
setting yourself up for frustration at best and failure at worst.

*Don't be afraid to set a higher level of commitment and ex-
pectation for the group than seems comfortable.* The idea that
setting a high bar scares people away is a myth. Playing it safe

and leading with a low bar of expectation usually results in mediocrity. Most folks would rather do something better with their time than meander through a mediocre group. If you paint a compelling picture of the destination, the group will usually rise to the occasion, and it will pay big dividends over the course of your time together.

Many leaders avoid these conversations in the interest of playing it safe. As a result, they sacrifice transformation for momentary comfort. It is okay if everyone in the group doesn't seem as committed initially or doesn't agree on everything. The discussion itself builds trust with your group members, breaks the ice for those that don't really want to be there, and gets the important expectations out in the open. The alternative—not knowing where you are going—will definitely not be helpful in the long run.

• • •

Practical Group Application

So, what's the nitty-gritty of putting this Core Component into practice? In one of your early times together—we suggest the first or second meeting—take the time to unpack your group expectations and determine your destination. Remember, knowing where you're going helps you get there. Most expectations for

MOST EXPECTATIONS FOR GROUPS FALL INTO THE CATEGORIES OF RELATIONSHIPS AND SPIRITUAL GROWTH.

groups fall into the categories of Relationships and Spiritual Growth. For each of these two categories, first invite everyone to share their thoughts and ideas. For example, you could ask "What do we want our relationships to look like in a year?" You can write them up on a flipchart like Stuart did, use sticky notes, write it down in an app on your phone, or whatever method fits your group. The technique is just a means to an end.

RELATIONAL EXPECTATIONS

Some group members may be looking for one other person who fully knows them. Some group members may want to improve their marriage. Some may simply want social friends while others might be looking to build a life-long community—the type of friends where their kids call their friend "Uncle Corey," or where they don't have to knock when they visit each other's homes. Understanding everyone's expectations and hopes for relationships in the group is vital to the overall success.

SPIRITUAL GROWTH EXPECTATIONS

People join groups at all stages of their spiritual journey and for all kinds of reasons. Some people might not be a Christian at all and have little or no desire to grow spiritually. Others might see this as the primary source of their spiritual maturity or hope for deeper discipleship. That's okay. The richness that comes from various perspectives and faith walks has been a surprising blessing to many groups.

GROUP GOALS

Every small group has its own fingerprint. Don't worry if people have seemingly disparate ideas and preferences. Most groups will find a consensus on preferences without much drama. If people are being vague, ask clarifying questions and use more definitive words that you think may represent what they mean. The key here is deciding that you will get everyone's input at the beginning. Once everyone who's willing to participate has shared, start to combine ideas and thoughts until you can articulate where your group wants to go for each category. We suggest doing this in one to two sentences per category. Remember, less is more.

These group goals will serve as a north star for the group along the way, reminding you where you're headed. Leading your group through a discussion around preferences, expectations, and goals will help get everyone on the same page from the beginning and give them an immediate internal answer to the question "Why am I going to group this week?"

Leader Resources

~∞∞∞∞∞~

At *trueface.org/cureforgroups* you'll find additional resources like the **Destination Planner** for capturing notes, and then use the one-page **Group Map** to record your group goals. The **Group Map** will provide a reference for your group as you go through this process.

Reflection Questions

1 Why did you decide to lead a group?

2 If you've been in a group before, as a member or a leader, what were your expectations going in? Were those met?

3 What do you hope your group feels like a year from now?

№ 02

The Captain

LEAD WITH INTENTIONALITY AND VULNERABILITY

*"We cannot lead anyone farther than
we have been ourselves."*

—JOHN C. MAXWELL

If a ship is at sea and a storm hits, where do the sailors look? While some might look out at the waves or stare bewildered at the gathering clouds, most will look to the captain. Is she freaking out or does she seem calm? What orders is he giving? When things get rocky, you need a captain who can lead the way and show you what to do. A good captain knows how to hold the course despite heavy seas and strong opposing winds.

The same is true for your leadership in a group. The members will look to you and your example. Do you share honestly? Do you own your stuff? Are you real and authentic when life gets a little rocky? You set the tone for the rest of the group. If you want an exceptional, transformational group, who you are as a leader is key.

• • •

El Felix Restaurant, Sunday Night, 7:30 p.m.

"Honestly, it's amazing. Her personality comes out more every day. Or maybe changes every day," Leslie laughed, shoving another tortilla chip in the salsa.

"I remember that stage," Tim shook his head. "It's somehow really incredible and incredibly frustrating at the same time, isn't it?"

Stuart leaned back. "Gosh, it's good to be around you two again. You're always so honest. It makes me feel better about myself."

Jane laughed, taking a sip of her drink. "If you can't be honest about how infuriating your kids are sometimes, you'll go crazy."

The waitress brought them their third bowl of chips. El Felix was Tim and Jane's favorite restaurant mainly because of their chips and salsa. Stuart and Leslie had asked the older couple if they could grab dinner and get some advice.

Tim redirected. "So, Stuart, you said you wanted to pick our brains about something."

"Yeah, well, we had our first group meeting. And . . . ," Stuart started. Then he looked at Leslie.

"And I won't speak for Stuart, but it felt a little rough." Leslie sighed. "We did that exercise you suggested, and it was helpful, I think. I feel like we got to a good place in the end. Maybe. But it was like pulling teeth to get people to talk."

"Wait, was this your *first* time meeting together?" Jane asked.

Leslie nodded. "Ah," she leaned back, glancing at Tim, "we may have steered you wrong there. Your first meeting probably should have just been a general get-to-know-you, social hangout. Then, the next time—your first "real" meeting—is a great time to do that group goals exercise. Sorry about that."

"Honestly, I feel like a hangout night might have been just as awkward at this point," Stuart shook his head. "I don't know what I was expecting, but it seemed like nobody really wanted to be there. It wasn't ten minutes before I wanted to say, 'Why are you guys even here?!'"

"Sounds like you weren't the only nervous ones. You know, you could have asked them why they showed up," Jane said. "Might have shaken everyone up in a good way."

Stuart laughed halfheartedly. "I almost did."

"Interesting. So why didn't you?" Tim asked, leaning in.

Stuart thought for a moment. "Well, I guess because that didn't feel very *Christian*. Does that make any sense?"

Jane smiled and leaned back. "Oh, it does. But I think that might be part of the issue. How did the two of you feel during the meeting?"

"I couldn't remember the last time I'd felt that awkward," Stuart replied. "But, in the same moment, I hoped I appeared confident, like I knew what I was doing."

"Seriously?" Leslie frowned. "You didn't appear awkward at all. You seemed like you were in your element, and I was thankful at least one of us was because I felt middle school awkward."

"You two are always so honest with us. Why did you feel like you couldn't be real with the group?" Tim asked as he scraped the last of the guac.

Now it was Leslie's turn to think for a moment. "I mean,

we were trying to be good leaders. And I guess I feel like good leaders know what's going on . . . right?"

Tim and Jane looked at each other and smiled. "Yes, that's how some people define a good leader—always composed, always confident. But, we don't believe that," Jane said.

"We really don't," Tim added. "We've learned over our years that as goes the leader, so goes the group. If you have any hopes of a group that's real and honest then you, both of you, have to lead with that foot, so to speak. If you aren't being real, don't expect them to be."

"Vulnerability is the secret sauce to find what you are looking for," Jane said. "They'll follow your lead. You set the stage. If you want an authentic, deep group, then be authentic and deep. If you want your group to be somewhere safe enough that people can share the raw stuff of their lives, then share the raw stuff of *your* lives. You have to model that for them."

WE CANNOT LET SOMEONE LOVE US UNLESS WE TRUST THEM.

Stuart asked with a puzzled look, "Yeah, I see why vulnerability is important, but I don't necessarily see why it's *that* important."

Jane smiled and leaned forward. "Vulnerability is trusting others with the real you. We cannot let someone love us unless we trust them. See, we all have innate needs for things like security, acceptance, and belonging. Trusting others means allowing them to see those needs and then allowing them to help meet them. Letting someone see your needs is what it means to be vulnerable. When we let someone *meet* our needs, that is what it means to receive love. When we choose to not be vulnerable, we're saying, 'I don't need you.' That's the language of a wounded heart, not a healthy one.[7] Vulnerability isn't easy. It takes courage to trust others with the real you, needs and all. But, if you'll go there, it allows you to be more known and more loved. *That* is why vulnerability is so important."

"Don't miss that, you two. What Jane just said is the key," Tim spread his hands out on the table. "You have such a cool opportunity to help create an environment like that, and it starts with *your* courage to be vulnerable with them, to trust them with the real you. You can't expect your group to go where you aren't willing to go yourself. Will it always go well? Definitely not. Will being vulnerable sometimes backfire on you? Sure. But it's either risk that for a real, authentic, life-giving group,

> **YOU CAN'T EXPECT YOUR GROUP TO GO WHERE YOU AREN'T WILLING TO GO YOURSELF.**

or keep playing around in the shallow end wondering why you're bored." Tim shrugged. "Sorry if that's blunt, but it's true."

Stuart thought for a moment. "Huh, I want to keep unpacking that, but now that I look back I can see how you and Jane did that with our group all those years ago. You went first. Made it feel less scary. And I have always really felt loved by the two of you." He thought for another moment. "To be honest though, going first *does* feel kinda scary."

"Scary I can do," Leslie said, "but not boring." Tim and Jane looked at each other and grinned.

What You Just Saw

This Core Component of leading with intentionality and vulnerability is the most pivotal of the five Components. To really understand this one though, we have to dig down deeper—all the way, in fact, to the bedrock of who we are.

There is another principle at play here, undergirding this Core Component and stretching throughout our lives: *Who you are is more important than what you do.* Understanding and applying this principle will change every aspect of your life. Think we're overstating? Stay with me and read this section slowly.

This principle begs the question, "Who am I?" For the Christ follower, it also begs the question, "Who is God?" as we believe that he is the ultimate authority on our identity. These are foundational questions for all of us and your daily life reflects your answer to them, whether it's conscious or not. The answer to that question has ripple effects that can be felt far and wide. *Especially* if you're a leader.

If you really examine your life, do you feel connected to people around you but not really that *close* to them? Do you feel like most of your friends know a lot *about* you, but don't know the *real you*? If you're really honest with yourself, do you actually feel like what you do is more important than who you are?

The reality is that it's just safer and easier to keep relationships at a relatively shallow depth. Unfortunately, in doing so we miss out on deeper connection and intimacy. The result is that we feel like people know us but don't *really* know us. As a result, they may love us but not *really* love us.

So, what's actually going on here? One word—shame.

Remember, shame is what keeps us at stage two friendship

and makes us afraid of moving into the deep friendship of stage three. Shame tells us that we have to fake it because who we really are—our true identity—is ugly and messed up. Sure, we believe God gave us salvation and wiped the slate clean, but now he's waiting for us to meet him in the middle and prove that we're willing to put in the work. Unfortunately, most of us don't feel like we're doing a very good job. We still sin, think terrible thoughts, and feel embarrassed by some of our destructive patterns. We don't want anyone to know that we're still struggling, so we pretend like we're farther along than we feel. We fake it 'til we make it, and we're pretty sure God is disappointed that we haven't progressed as quickly as he'd like. Surely he cares more about what we do than who we are.

Do you see how identity, *how I see myself*, and theology, *how I see God*, get all wrapped up in each other? If we see God with his arms crossed, tapping his foot as we try to prove to him how serious we are about our faith, then our identity is that we are disappointments. We're just sorry old sinners who can't get our act together. Conversely, if we see ourselves as messed up degenerates, then our theology says that God must see us the same way. Our warped view of ourselves begins to warp our view of God.

I literally sighed as I wrote that last sentence. So many of us—myself included—have been caught up in the lies of shame for years.

SINNER OR SAINT?

Let's unpack this. If I view God as both the loving Father and righteous Judge, I can begin believing that he actually has taken care of my sin so that he can draw me close. If I believe that he really did make me into a new—*actually new*—creation when I accepted Jesus,[8] then I no longer see myself as a saved sinner. I am a saint, who still sins.[9] Sound like semantics? It's not.

If I believe I'm a sinner striving to become a saint, I'm back trying to pull myself up by my bootstraps. I will get more and more discouraged with every misstep, sin, and unholy thought. It means I need to hide who I fear I am and work to change who I believe I am. What I do is more important than who I am. Or, put another way, *what I do will turn me into who I want to be.* Sadly, I believe the same about other people—they just need to try harder and get their act together. This often leads to a great lack of compassion and empathy, both for myself and for others.

If, on the other hand, I'm a saint who still sins, then even though I still have sinful behaviors I will know they don't define who I truly am, because who I truly am is a beloved, delighted in, holy, and righteous child of my smiling Father God. It will take my lifetime for the truth of my new self to work its way through all my behaviors, patterns, and wounds. Those behaviors *do not* define me. Who *God* says I am defines me. This allows me to see other believers as maturing saints as well.

I NO LONGER SEE MYSELF AS A SAVED SINNER. I AM A SAINT, WHO STILL SINS.

Do you see how this can change our relationships and especially change a group dynamic? It means that we get to remind each other of who we really are instead of trying to fix each other. We get to remind each other—ourselves included—of this principle: Who we are (saints) is more important than what we do (sin). As Pete Scazzero confirms, "Leadership is not always being the strong one; it is being the weak one who is made strong by God alone." [10]

Are you with me? From my unhealthy perspective, who I really am doesn't deserve to be loved. I need to hide. But from God's perspective, who I really am is glorious. I can risk letting others see my true face. An accurate theology and identity gradually strip away the power of shame in our lives. When shame hisses that you can't possibly tell anyone *that* messed up thing because they'll find out who you really are and reject you, we can stop shame in its tracks. "I know who I really am," we can respond. "I am a fully transformed saint. I am beloved and enjoyed and holy. I still have lots of rough edges and patterns that I need help with. Yes, they could judge me and reject me, but that doesn't change who I am. Jesus has already secured my identity on my best day, my worst day, and every day in between." [11]

• • •

Why This Matters in Groups

This second Core Component of leading with intentionality and vulnerability means that who you are as the leader is absolutely key for building an amazing, life-changing group. It can be easy to hear that and think, "Great, now I just have to be this totally healthy, mature, real, authentic, vulnerable leader. My group is going to fail, and it's all going to be my fault."

Is your leadership important? Absolutely. But God has a tendency to specifically use what we see as the worst things about us to reveal himself to others. So, breathe.

Practically, every group has a leader. The leader has the greatest impact on the culture of the group. If your group doesn't have an official leader, I bet there is someone everyone naturally looks to or who has adopted the role unofficially. If you are that unofficial leader or have a passion to help influence the effectiveness of your group, don't run away from that opportunity.

As the captain of your group, you are going to set the stage with how you see yourself and how you see God. That is why this is so important for you to dig into. If shame is still in charge, you won't be real with your group. You'll share safe struggles. You'll keep it light and only relate at a surface level in order to protect yourself. If you are slowly learning to reject shame and instead hold fast to who Jesus says you are, you'll be able to be vulnerable, honest, and real. You will give your group the gift of opening the door for them to be their true selves, warts and all. The gift will return to you as your leadership becomes increasingly authentic.

IF YOU ARE SLOWLY LEARNING TO REJECT SHAME AND INSTEAD HOLD FAST TO WHO JESUS SAYS YOU ARE, YOU'LL BE ABLE TO BE VULNERABLE, HONEST, AND REAL.

Ruth Haley-Barton writes, "This is the kind of truth that ultimately sets us free to lead from a truer self."[12]

As leaders, we build a room of grace for our group by modeling vulnerability, which is trusting God and our group members with our true selves. This isn't for the fainthearted. Choosing to trust others with your whole person and choosing to be stretched in order to invite your group to be vulnerable requires courage, and the freedom you experience by being fully known is amazing. That freedom is attractive and infectious. This is how you create a high trust environment of grace for others. One warning: Once you experience this level of trust and authenticity, you'll be ruined for anything less, and so will your group.

Now, I want to be candid. This kind of vulnerability opens you up to the possibility of being hurt. One of my friends calls it "handing them the bullets." It gives others the kind of access that could be used to hurt you. Being an intentional and vulnerable captain takes courage. Someone might not feel comfortable with the fact that you struggle with (fill in the blank). A person who is insecure in their own identity may withdraw or even respond with judgment. But, if you shrink back from trust for fear of what might happen, you'll inadvertently create an environment where people will have a limited experience with love and freedom. In contrast, if you receive it without fear no matter how a group member responds, you will nurture the group's trust of each other.

If you have experienced the freedom of being fully known, then you know that freedom and vulnerability are inseparable. You know it's totally worth the risk.

Let's head back to seeing how Leslie and Stuart navigate this, and then we'll walk you through a practical group application.

• • •

7 Attributes of Exceptional Leaders

- **Model Vulnerability:** Choose to trust others in the group with your person—the person beyond the mask. Trust them with the good, the bad, and the ugly.

- **Follow Feelings:** When feelings are shared, pursue them as the gateway to the heart and the catalyst for connection.

- **Ask Questions:** Follow up with a second question ("Tell me more.") and third question ("It sounds like you felt . . . ").

- **Speak Less:** Be quick to listen and slow to speak. When tempted to fix, don't jump in. Instead, ask further questions to increase your understanding. When people feel understood, they feel trusted. People feel understood with active listening, like reflection and further open-ended questions.

- **Serve People in the Group:** Be a model of servant leadership by looking for opportunities to serve each other.

- **Lead with Intentionality:** Are you reactive or proactive as a facilitator?

- **Pray:** Pray for the people in your group and listen for the subtle guidance of the Holy Spirit.

Stuart and Leslie's Living Room, Thursday Night, 7:00 p.m.

As everyone settled into their seats the following Thursday, Leslie took the lead. "Alright, last week we talked about why we want to do this group and what we want it to look like. Honestly? That was hard for me. I've never led a group before. Neither has Stuart. I felt like I needed to pretend to know what I was doing, but the truth is that I was making it up as I went. Faker, right here." She pointed a finger at herself.

"You did a great job, Leslie," Dwayne reassured her. "And you seemed fine to us."

"Yeah well, that's kind of the problem," Leslie leaned forward a little. "Remember our first group goal? 'To have real relationships where we live life together and truly know and trust each other'? Pretending like I have it all together is lightyears from being real. Instead, here's the deal—I'm going to try to not do that. Emphasis on *try*."

Keisha gave her a knowing smile. "I get what you're saying, Les. It's hard. But we appreciate you sharing that." The group murmured their agreement.

"And, in the spirit of sharing," Stuart picked up, "we thought it might be helpful to share parts of our stories with each other over the next few weeks. Now, ideally it'd have been great if we could have planned a weekend getaway and shared our stories sitting outside by a quiet lake drinking lattes or something. Those mentors we told you about, Tim and Jane, told us how powerful a getaway can be, but obviously we didn't plan that far ahead."

"How dare you," Keisha teased.

Stuart laughed. He took a deep breath, reminding himself

what Jane had told them. "You are a fully transformed, maturing, beloved saint. That's never going to change. That means you can risk being real because God—not other people's opinions—has defined who you are."

He glanced at Leslie, who seemed to know what he was thinking and gave him a reassuring smile. "I'll go first then, since it was my idea. Like Leslie said, I don't want to be the kind of leader that pretends like everything's fine, because it's not. I've got my issues. Thankfully, I've also got a God that loves me like crazy and a wife that has my back, so I think I'm going to be okay."

There was a ripple of laughter.

"We'll set a timer. Twenty minutes for each of us," Leslie added, getting out her phone. "Just so we don't accidentally keep going for an hour."

"You know me well," Stuart laughed. The room fell silent as Leslie set the timer and Stuart gathered his thoughts, running a hand through his hair, which was his telltale sign he was nervous.

YOU ARE A FULLY TRANSFORMED, MATURING, BELOVED SAINT. THAT'S NEVER GOING TO CHANGE.

Leslie gave him a thumbs-up. "Alright, well, I actually didn't grow up here. I grew up in Illinois and lived there until I was ten."

Stuart walked them through some of the bigger pieces of his life. He talked about his parents—his mom who was incredibly sweet but also unwilling to defend him against his dad. His dad's anger issues, which sometimes turned violent. How he started sneaking out, just so he could feel like he had some space and freedom from his own home.

His voice cracked a little when he told them about how poorly he handled a pregnancy scare with a high school girlfriend.

It didn't help that Erik's expression had a good amount of disappointment on it, and maybe some confusion. *He's probably wondering why he would be in a group led by a guy like me,* Stuart's mind raced. He breathed, reminding himself, *God already knows all of this, and He loves me. Leslie knows and she loves me. It's okay if Erik thinks less of me right now. It's worth giving other people some space to be real.*

He took them through his time reconnecting with Jesus after years of trying to run, and how meeting Leslie (and her refusal to initially go out with him) was part of what made him start to change. He brought them all the way to the present, to how he loved his two little girls more than he could have imagined, but how these preschool years sometimes gave him that same "I've got to get out of here" feeling he had as a teenager.

"And that's kind of where I am now," he shrugged, looking at Leslie.

"19:37. Nice." Leslie showed him the timer, grinning.

The group fell silent again, but it was less tense than before. It felt thoughtful. "Man, thanks for sharing," Dwayne spoke up, squeezing Keisha's hand. "I've known you for a few years, but I never knew a lot of that. Especially the stuff with your dad. That's rough. Thanks for letting us in on that."

Everyone else nodded in agreement.

"When you think about how you felt trapped in high school, was there anyone that felt safe for you?" Keisha asked.

"Great question," he paused for a moment. "You know my tenth grade English teacher actually comes to mind. He was always for me and became someone who I trusted." Stuart explained how the teacher had noticed things he was good at and encouraged him in them, and how that was the first time he really started thinking about what he wanted to do in the future.

"Thanks for listening and for the questions, guys. Leslie, you want to go next?"

Leslie took a deep breath and cracked her knuckles. "Might as well. Here, you hold the timer."

Co-leaders

I realized the power of co-leaders in group therapy. The outcomes of therapeutic groups with a co-therapist were so much higher than when I led by myself. With a co-leader, you can model healthy relationships, lean into each other's strengths, play off of each other, and have the blessing of having a co-laborer alongside you.

If you are in a couple's group, many times your spouse will be a natural co-leader, but I also recommend having another couple co-lead with you. If you are in a men's, women's, or mixed group, have a co-leader! Your shared leadership will be lighter, more fun, and more encouraging. You aren't the whole package; leverage gifts of another person to become a more complete duo.

Practical Group Application

Applying this Core Component of leading with intentionality and vulnerability to your group can be done many different ways. It's also important to note that this is an ongoing application. We naturally slide toward hiding (thanks, Adam and Eve). Therefore, revisit this often with your group.

The application we suggest is to set aside time for sharing your stories with each other early on. This invites everyone to come to the table with some vulnerability and allows your group to begin building the foundational blocks of trust as you let each other know more of who you really are.

Besides prioritizing the time to share each of your stories, it's important that you as the leader give the gift of going first. If you share your story with a high degree of vulnerability, you open the door for others to do likewise. If you share your story and it's all safe stuff, then that is exactly what you're going to get back. If you risk letting the group know more of your real stories, the ones that are sometimes messy or difficult to tell, then you invite the rest of the group to follow you into deeper waters. Not all will go with you, and that's okay. But, by going first and by sharing with genuine vulnerability, you set the tone for the group.

There are three questions you need to ask as the captain of this group. The first is very practical: *What is our plan for sharing stories and building trust?* There are a few options below to help you think through it. Building trust is unfortunately like swimming upstream; without intentional effort you'll drift downstream toward shallow pools of comfort. Prioritize building authentic, vulnerable relationships, and make a plan.

The second question is personal: *Am I ready to move past the shame barrier and model vulnerability?* This is a good question to ponder with God and with anyone else you deeply trust. You don't need to be ready to share your deepest, darkest secrets with strangers. Trust takes time to build. However, you can accelerate relational connection by choosing to trust others and taking the courageous next step of becoming more known. Risk sharing some real, honest, difficult things in the confidence of who God says you are. Fight the temptation to pose and invite the group into a more authentic relationship where they get to know the real you. Are you willing?

> YOU CAN ACCELERATE RELATIONAL CONNECTION BY CHOOSING TO TRUST OTHERS

The last question should be revisited regularly in your group: *Are we continuing to increase our trust in each other?* Remember, vulnerable relationships don't continue that way without intentional effort. Have an ongoing conversation about this aspect of your group so you can continue pursuing depth when the current of shallow relationships tries to draw you away.

OPTIONS:

There are more options than these, but here are two ideas to get you started.

Option One: Plan a weekend getaway or an overnight trip together. Have relaxed hang out time, but also set aside time for each person to share their story. Getting away from normal life can help people open up in new ways.

Option Two: Set aside two meetings in a row for everyone to share their stories for fifteen to twenty minutes. Decide ahead of time who will share at each meeting so everyone can feel prepared. A specific plan for Option 2 is found in *Embark: A Six-Part Study to Launch your Group.*

GUIDELINES:

- Set an expectation of fifteen to twenty minutes with a timer.
- Give them a signal when they have five minutes left.
- Allow five to ten minutes for questions and heartfelt responses.

 Tip: Timers work, especially for sharing stories during a normal group time. As soon as the first person shares for fifty minutes, rambling as they try to remember their childhood dog's name, you will immediately remember this tip and wish you had started with a timer. Keep in mind your specific group variables. Less time to share is often appropriate for groups that plan to be together for a shorter duration. Also, I have seen breakthroughs happen during a retreat setting where there was more time and space for each person to share. I didn't use a timer in that environment, but I did set expectations and asked people to try to wrap it up when needed.

Leader Resources

~~∞∞∞∞~~

Use the **Sharing Your Story Guide** and other resources at *trueface.org/cureforgroups* to prepare for practicing vulnerability in your group." Look at the leader commitment on your **Group Map** for a reminder of how you want to lead your group with vulnerability. For more guidance in preparing to tell your story, check out *Embark: A Six-Part Study to Launch Your Group.*

Reflection Questions

1 What is the greatest extent of vulnerability you have experienced with someone else? Was it a positive or negative experience?

2 What are the primary fears you have about being more
vulnerable with your group?

3 Do you primarily see yourself as a sinner that is striving
to become a saint or a saint who still sins? How does
that affect your daily life?

Nº 03

The Crew

CLARIFY YOUR GROUP CULTURE

"If you do not manage culture, it manages you."

—EDGAR SCHEIN

You can have a great destination and a strong, selfless captain, but if you have a mistrusting, conflict-prone crew, your chances of a successful voyage are pretty slim. If no one's sure what their role is, what the rules are, or how they're supposed to interact with each other, every task is going to feel like an uphill battle instead of a smooth, coordinated operation. You'll spend more time mediating tense interactions than sailing. Establishing your crew's culture is vital.

Rest assured, sooner or later you're going to face some conflict. Someone's going to talk about one member's struggle outside of the group, or another might begin to dominate the conversation by telling others what they should do or think.

Things can go sideways quickly if you don't take time to clarify the values and commitments of your group.

· · ·

Stuart and Leslie's Patio, Thursday, 7:45 p.m.

"Thanks for sharing, Keisha," Leslie said warmly as Keisha finished sharing her story. Over the last two weeks, almost everyone had shared, and Leslie was encouraged at how open people tried to be. It felt like they were making little deposits of trust in each other and slowly opening up to form real bonds.

"Does anyone have any prayer requests before we close tonight?" Stuart asked, pulling out a notepad.

Keisha shared about a work presentation she had coming up that she was nervous about, and Erik asked for prayer for his aunt who had recently been diagnosed with an aggressive cancer.

"Anyone else?" Stuart asked, looking around.

"Um," Amy began, eyes on her own notebook. Leslie felt herself go still. Amy never shared voluntarily. She frowned at her hands. "I'm not really sure how to put it. I've just been feeling . . . kind of numb, I guess?" She shrugged, still not looking at any of them. "Like, spiritually. I don't want to read my Bible. I don't really want to go to church. I just feel . . . yeah, numb, I guess. So, prayers for that would be good."

Leslie took a deep breath as she thought to herself, *Wow, that was honest, and raw, and . . . sacred.* Just as she was opening her mouth to say so, Melissa jumped in.

"Amy, do you think there is something you need to re-pent of?" Melissa asked. "I feel like usually when we're feeling apathetic like that, it means there's something in our lives that we need to repent of, something that's separating us from God. Have you thought about that?"

Leslie felt like a horse had kicked her in the stomach. Here was Amy, spreading her vulnerable wings, and Melissa just completely shot her down.

"Um . . . nothing that I know of, but maybe." Leslie could sense Amy retreating back into herself.

"Well, you should pray about it," Melissa prescribed. "In the Psalms—I forget which one—David asks God to search his heart. Here, let me find it." She started flipping through her Bible, and Leslie could feel her blood begin to boil.

"I don't think we need that, Melissa," Leslie blurted out. "Amy's not asking for us to quote scripture at her right now."

Melissa raised her eyebrows at Leslie, clearly offended. "Wow, okay. I was just looking for something from God's Word to help. I would think that's what we should always be sharing with each other."

"Well, yes, but . . . ," Leslie trailed off and took a deep breath. "Sorry, Melissa I didn't mean to offend you. I just—feel like we should move on."

And just like that, all the built-up trust in the room got sucked out. Leslie had never experienced vertigo before, but she swore a case was coming on fast.

"Okay," Stuart resumed bravely. "I'll, um, pray for us then."

Mountain Coffee Co., Saturday Morning, 9:30 a.m.

"It was terrible," Leslie moaned, her head on the table. She raised her head and looked at Tim and Jane, thoroughly defeated. "It was going so well. People were opening up. And then Melissa jumped in and tried to fix Amy. And then I jumped in and made everything worse."

"I'm sure it wasn't as bad as you think it was," Jane said soothingly.

"Ask him! It was bad," she replied, motioning to Stuart.

Stuart squinted at the ceiling, possibly hoping for divine intervention of some kind. "I mean . . . well . . . yes, okay, it was pretty painful. Sorry, Les." He gave her an apologetic smile. "But at least you tried to do *something*. I completely froze and would have just let Melissa run right over her because I didn't know what to say."

Leslie moaned again. "Help us. What should we have done instead? How could we have avoided it—or at least handled it better?"

"Man, you guys, that's hard," Tim replied empathetically. "We've been there, and there's no getting around the fact that it's just plain *hard*. Maybe give yourselves a little grace because there's no easy answer here. We can't teach you some magic words that will stop that from ever happening again or what will always be the right thing to say. Every situation's a little different."

"Okay, but throw us a bone here, Tim. Something!" Leslie pleaded. Tim and Jane laughed.

"Something we've done that's helped is to adopt some values and make commitments as a group," Jane answered. "It's kind of like that exercise we had you do with the group goals—it's a way for everyone to agree together how we're going to treat each other, what the culture of the group is going to be. And then, when someone 'breaks' one of those commitments," she held up air quotes, "you have an easier way to address it. Notice I didn't say *easy*, just *easier* because you can gently remind them of what you all decided together."

"Can you give us an example?" Stuart asked. "I'm a card-carrying conflict avoider. It's going to be hard for me to speak up."

"Well, in light of your last, uh, interaction, you may need to address it a little more directly," Tim nodded toward Leslie. "I know you'll probably roll your eyes at this, but this could turn out to be a really good thing for your group." Leslie pointed to her eyes and rolled them, but Tim plowed on. "I mean it. This

> **WHEN WE DO CONFLICT WELL, IT CAN ACTUALLY BRING US A LOT CLOSER TOGETHER.**

is another chance to be real. Not just about your own stuff, but about a dynamic in the group. When we do conflict well, it can actually bring us a lot closer together."

"Or drive a bloody stake in the heart of our group," Leslie pointed out.

Tim smiled. "If I know anything about you, Leslie, it's that you're willing to walk through fire for people you care about. I'm not worried."

"You might start with addressing it just with Melissa," Jane picked up. "Give her a call this week. Apologize sincerely. See if you can come together on that. And then, at your next meeting, share with the group that you two talked and that you apologized. That way they know that it isn't just being avoided."

"Then I'd bring up values and commitments. You can simply say, 'Now that we've been meeting together awhile, we wanted to talk about what values we have as a group and what commitments we want to make about how we treat each other.' Then just go around the room and talk about it. Maybe think about a few ahead of time to get the ball rolling. One commitment could be that if someone brings something vulnerable to the table, the group just honors that and doesn't try to fix them unless they *specifically ask for advice*. You can word it in a way that isn't calling out Melissa—because you're not."

"And if it happens again?" Leslie asked.

"Like I said, not easy," Jane shook her head, "but at least you will have common language. Once you have your group commitments lined up, it will only be a matter of time before someone goes off course. When it happens, trust your judgement and listen to the Holy Spirit for the best way to respond in love. Your response will be different every time."

Jane continued, "It could look like thanking the person for the comment and redirecting. It could look like saying, 'Before we unpack that, I might be wrong, but Amy might just need us to listen to her on this one. I want to make sure we—myself included—avoid slipping into fix it mode. I don't know why I do that, but I want to *only* offer advice when it's asked for.'"

Tim chimed in. "It could look like discussing the situation afterwards one-on-one with the person. Leadership isn't easy, but the key factor is that if you've talked about it as a group, you will have a baseline of relational commitments to call everyone back to—including yourself."

"Okay, we can do that," Stuart nodded at Leslie. "Any other commitments or values you two have found helpful?"

Relationship Killers

Here are some relational dynamics that often derail a group. Reading through this list may help you think proactively about what values and commitments you'd like to bring up.

- Dominating the conversation.
- Not adhering to confidentiality.
- Using sarcasm.
- Gossiping.
- Not prioritizing the group or the relationships.
- Not being emotionally present at group, even if physically present.
- Judging each other.
- Trying to fix each other.
- Preaching more than asking questions.

Relationship Healers

~⌒∞∞∞∞∞⌒~

Active and reflective listening are skills that take practice. They are incredibly important in creating relational connections in a group and building trust. Active and reflective listening techniques include:

- Demonstrating concern.

- Paraphrasing to show understanding.

- Using nonverbal cues which show understanding such as nodding, eye contact, and leaning forward.

- Brief verbal affirmations like "I hear you," "I know," "Sure," "Thank you," or "I understand."

- Asking open-ended questions.

- Asking specific questions to seek clarification.

- Waiting to disclose your opinion.

. . .

Stuart and Leslie's Patio, Thursday Night, 5:30 p.m.

"Melissa, I'm so sorry," Leslie sighed. "I didn't handle that well. Stuart and I kind of get into this recurring argument where I feel like . . . ," Leslie stopped herself. This wasn't about her. "No, scratch that. I shouldn't have talked to you like that, period, and especially in front of the group. I just want to say that I'm so sorry."

Melissa nodded, taking a sip of her water. She seemed to have two modes—talking too much or completely withdrawing. Clearly she was in withdrawing mode right now. "Thanks. I appreciate that."

Leslie fell silent, unsure of what else to say. She had asked if Melissa would come over a little early this week so they could talk before everyone else arrived.

Melissa swirled her water, watching it. After another span of silence, she said, "Mike has told me before, 'Please, no verses.' But I don't get it. I'm just trying to help."

Leslie nodded. She had to bite back her knee jerk response. Instead, she took a deep breath. "That would be hard to hear, when you're trying to do something good and it isn't being seen that way. . ."

Melissa frowned at her water. "Yeah. Thanks." After another few moments she squinted out at the darkening sky. "Do you and Stuart struggle with this?"

Leslie sighed. Be yourself. Be honest. "We do. We're both fixers actually, so it's not that I don't like when he's trying to help. But sometimes I just want to feel like someone understands, I guess. And . . . ," she tried to think of the right words for how it felt. Melissa had turned toward her, watching her face intently. "And I guess . . . I want to know that he's okay with me being not okay. If I'm sad, I want to know that he loves me and that he's okay if I'm sad or scared or whatever. We've both had to learn we don't need to fix each other to love each other. Does that make any sense?"

Melissa turned back forward, looking out at the yard. She didn't say a word. *Was that too much?* Leslie wondered, but forced herself to take a deep breath in and out. The sun continued to sink lower, the last bit just peeking out over the horizon as they sat in more silence, though it was less uncomfortable than before. Melissa's voice was quiet as she kept her eyes on the horizon, "I wonder if that's how Mike feels."

She glanced back over at Leslie, as if a little unsure if it was safe to say that. Leslie gave her a small smile and shrugged again. "You could ask him."

• • •

Two Hours Later

Leslie gave everyone time to get settled in their seats, and then she spoke up. "Okay, the easy thing would be to let the past be the past and just keep moving forward. But we initially committed to something that we all admitted wouldn't be easy. So, here it goes. I hated how our last time together ended."

Every eye in the room was fixed on Leslie. Nobody moved.

"Amy shared some vulnerable feelings with us. Melissa responded in a way that made me uncomfortable. I didn't really know what to do, so I jumped on Melissa, strong armed the conversation, and essentially shut it down. Remember?"

Everyone nodded. Erik smiled and said, "Not exactly a train wreck, but close."

Leslie sighed, "Yes, it was. It was unfair to Melissa. To Amy, too. I wanted you to know that Melissa and I have talked since then. I'm grateful she was willing to meet with me. I had some unspoken expectations about how we would treat one another

64

in this group. Melissa didn't know them, Amy didn't, none of you did. I still acted out of those expectations, and things went sideways. I've already apologized to Melissa. Amy, I'm sorry. You didn't need me to rescue you. You're an adult. And I want to apologize to the rest of you as well."

Melissa gave Leslie a small smile. "Thanks for saying that, Leslie."

"But here's the deal. If our expectations stay unspoken, we'll just keep having collisions like that. It's inevitable. That's why we thought we could spend some time tonight getting some of our expectations out on the table? Or the flipchart?" Leslie's glance at Stuart was met with a grin.

"I'm in," Stuart said. "Anybody else?"

"I like it," Erik responded. "You're basically talking about establishing ground rules, right?"

"Kind of. More like, commitments of how we want to treat each other. I like that better than the word 'rules.'" Leslie shrugged.

"Hear, hear!" Mike replied, getting a chuckle from the rest of the group.

Leslie smiled, "Glad you're on my team, Mike. Stuart and I felt it would be good to discuss group values at some point—values describing how we want this group to *feel*. But maybe making some group commitments will naturally cover values as well."

"I can go first," Stuart offered. "For me, it's really important that no one tries to, I don't know, preach at me. I want us to be learning together on the same level, you know? I get enough instruction from my bosses and on Sunday—that's not what I want from you guys. Because of that, I'd want us to commit to no preaching. Thoughts?"

"Agreed, Stuart. For me it's really important that I trust that whatever I say here stays here," Erik ventured. "I've been in a group before where some of the hard stuff I was sharing leaked out to others and turned into gossip. My ex-wife and I were separated at the time, and to have our dirty laundry shared like that . . . ," he said as he shook his head. "Nope. I was done."

Stuart cringed, "Ugh. I'm sorry, Erik. That's rough." He stood and wrote on the chart, "Group Commitments: #1. No Preaching. #2. No Leaking."

"How about no fixing?" Dwayne offered. "I know I've got my issues. I'm not here for you to fix them—I'm here for you to be alongside me in them."

"Dwayne, I wish I could say things half as succinctly as you do," Leslie shook her head.

"I like that," Amy said simply. Erik nodded too.

After some more discussion, Stuart stepped back. "Okay, so far we've got no fixing, no leaking, no preaching."

"What kind of leaking?" Mike asked, feigning suspicion. "Like no bathroom breaks?"

The men laughed and the women rolled their eyes. Stuart laughed the hardest, beyond pleased that Mike had just made a joke.

• • •

What You Just Saw

I think a lot of us have been in Leslie's position—and Melissa's, Amy's, and Stuart's for that matter. It is that awkward moment in a group where things suddenly go relationally sideways. Someone shuts down, powers up, or gets snippy. As Leslie said: "It's terrible." It's also guaranteed to happen when you put a bunch of humans together in the same room and try to get real.

There's an unspoken crew culture, or family system, in our board meetings, friend groups, and at our dinner tables. There are unspoken rules and expectations of how everyone behaves and interacts. "*Never* question the boss." "Don't bring up her daughter." "We don't argue openly in our house."

THERE'S AN UNSPOKEN CREW CULTURE, OR FAMILY SYSTEM, IN OUR BOARD MEETINGS, FRIEND GROUPS, AND AT OUR DINNER TABLES.

There's no getting away from the fact that we as humans create expectations in our relationships, and that's not necessarily a bad thing. But when these aren't discussed and agreed upon, things will inevitably go sideways at some point. That's why clarifying your crew culture is the third Core Component.

. . .

Why This Matters in Groups

Since a crew culture is inevitable, will you intentionally talk about and shape it together, or will you let it develop on its own, discovering the boundaries and issues only when you cross them? You can react to these dynamics or you can shape them on purpose. Normal groups react to the culture as it develops. Good groups have articulated values and commitments. *Transformational* groups reflect their values and live out their commitments. You, the captain, have an incredible opportunity to help create the crew culture in your group by opening up the conversation and guiding your group through choosing their values and commitments.

TRANSFORMATIONAL GROUPS REFLECT THEIR VALUES AND LIVE OUT THEIR COMMITMENTS.

Below we'll outline some practical guidelines on having this kind of conversation. But first, let's look at how this can get sideways. There are three ways that values and commitments become worthless, even after you've discussed them.

1. The leader does not model the values and commitments.

What if your boss insisted that you never interrupt people, but then consistently interrupted you? That "commitment" of not interrupting would feel worthless, hypocritical, or perhaps even manipulative. Don't let this integrity gap poison your group. Leaders should always ask themselves: "Am I modeling our group's values and living up to our commitments?" A group's culture will often reflect the leader. If you as the leader don't model the group dynamics, it doesn't have a shot.

2. Group members consistently break the commitments without redirection from someone else in the group.

This is often the most difficult to address. If you have commitments of "no leaking, no fixing, and no preaching," and somebody isn't following one of those guidelines, how do you lovingly call them out without "fixing" them? This is the art of healthy conflict. It's never easy. It takes empathy and insightful questions, and even the most experienced leader will sometimes get it wrong. The point is not to be perfect (you can't be), but instead the goal is to lean in and practice these skills of healthy conflict.

Often you can ask the person sharing if that was what they were looking for, or you can ask the person making the statement a follow up question about their intent. If a member of the group consistently fails to align with the values and commitments laid out by the group, meeting one-on-one afterwards is often a best practice. Take the interaction below as an example.

"Hey Erik, do you have a minute? I noticed a pattern during our time together. I'm not sure if you are aware of it, but I think it might actually be hindering what you're trying to accomplish. Can we talk about it?"

Erik might reply, "Uh, sure. What do you mean?"

"Ever since we started the group, I've noticed that you're very discerning and great at identifying opportunities to solve or address problems. You see it so quickly! I also know how much you care for and love others and have a desire to help them thrive. I've also noticed a few times now that you have shared in a way that solved someone's problem when they didn't ask for it to be solved. I've noticed this because I do the same thing, and it's so hard for me to not do that. I think this can come across as 'fixing,' which I don't think is your intention. I just wanted to run that by you and get your thoughts about how we can continue to move towards creating an environment where we can share openly and be more known."

3. Nobody remembers the values and commitments.

Strange, but true. It's amazing how easy it is for the agreed-up-on values and group commitments to fall by the wayside over time. It's wise to take a few minutes to realign the group around its values and commitments whenever there's a natural change or break in the calendar, like when you start up after some time off for the summer or whenever you're beginning a new curriculum. This can help you all keep the crew culture fresh in your minds.

• • •

Practical Group Application

One way to put this Core Component into practice is to use an exercise similar to what I suggested in Component One. This will have two sections: values and commitments.

VALUES

Another way of discussing values is to ask, "If someone came into our group in six months, how would we want them to describe us?" There are limitless options here. We've included some on the following page, and even more in *Embark*, which is the group study that pairs with this book. These are just starting points. Feel free to brainstorm your own or add to the list.

Have everyone in your group come up with their top three words that they would choose to describe your group's culture. You can write them down on a flip chart, put them all on index cards and spread them over a table, or use a shared note on your phones. Do whatever works for your group. Once everyone has shared their top three, look to see which ones you can combine. Then, have everyone vote on their top three choices until you get down to three to five descriptors or values for your group.

Values		
Safe	Serious	Purposeful
Intentional	Fun	Spontaneous
Vulnerable	Casual	Emotional
Transparent	Formal	Challenging
Focused	Timely	Welcoming

COMMITMENTS

Commitments are agreements on how you'll treat each other, kind of like agreed upon rules of operations for your group. A good commitment can be identified with an example of what it looks like when it happens, and an example when it doesn't. For example, "We don't leak," means, "What is shared in the group stays in the group." Said another way, "We commit to confidentiality." Confidentiality is a nonnegotiable for a healthy group. This should be clearly discussed and committed to by everyone in the group near the start

CONFIDENTIALITY IS A NONNEGOTIABLE FOR A HEALTHY GROUP.

of the group. When there is confidence that what is said never gets to hit the ears of anyone outside the group, you know your group has made that commitment their own.

Use the same system we outlined for values. Have everyone share their top ideas, and then combine and vote until you pare it down to three to five. Below are a few examples, but again, this isn't exhaustive. Feel free to create your own. Check out *Embark* for more ideas.

Commitments

We don't fix.	We look for ways to affirm each other.
We stand with each other.	We don't judge.
We commit to confidentiality.	We don't take ourselves too seriously.
We don't preach.	We look for ways to serve those around us.
We don't demean.	
We practice radical candor.	We don't veer from scripture.
We don't use sarcasm.	We don't ignore conflict.

The goal is to have three to five values and three to five commitments. These describe the group culture with aspirational and practical clarity that can serve as a guide for the group along the journey. It describes the feel aboard the ship, the relational environment shared by the other group members. By utilizing this Core Component of clarifying your group culture, you build in protection and intention for cultivating a trusting culture.

Leader Resources

~∞∞∞∞∞∞~

At *trueface.org/cureforgroups* you'll find additional resources. Use the **Crew Culture Brainstorm** to take notes for this discussion and add your group values and commitments to your **Group Map.**

Reflection Questions

1 What is a healthy culture you've experienced? What made it healthy?

2 What were some unspoken or spoken rules from your family of origin? Do you see the effects of that in your current life?

3 How do you usually deal with conflict? How might that affect your group?

The Ship

DESIGN YOUR TIME FOR TRANSFORMATION

"The alternative to good design is always bad design.
There is no such thing as no design."

—ADAM JUDGE

Ships are designed for specific purposes. A week aboard a tugboat would be a lousy way to spend a week in the Virgin Islands. Likewise, a sailing catamaran would never be able to push a 300-ton barge through the currents on the Mississippi, let alone help a 240,000-ton super tanker hold its position in a tide. Each type of vessel is designed from the keel up with its purpose and destination in mind.

The design of the ship deeply influences how the captain and crew spend their time on this adventure. While the destination may be exciting, the ship is where you actually live on your way there. The structure of your ship is what carries you toward your destination. In a very real sense, it holds you together.

So it goes with how we spend our time together in our group. Meeting together for sixty or ninety minutes once a week is not in and of itself a recipe for spiritual growth or authentic relationships. *How* you spend your time together is what carries you toward your destination. How you structure your time can either help or hinder your progress.

. . .

Stuart and Leslie's Living Room, Thursday Night, 7:45 p.m.

"I love that passage," Melissa sighed, shutting her Bible. Stuart put his phone down, closing his Bible app. They had just finished talking about Ephesians 4.

"So, any prayer requests?" Stuart asked as Leslie grabbed a notebook to write them down.

"Um," Mike frowned.

Mike has a prayer request? Stuart was amazed, and he tried to look nonchalant. "Well, it's not really a prayer request. I'm just, well, a little confused."

"With the passage?" Leslie asked.

"No, I get that. But the part about maturing, about no longer being babies but growing up in our faith—I don't really get how that's supposed to work. Like, is what we are doing here supposed to result in that?"

Stuart didn't immediately understand what Mike was getting at. "Can you tell us a little more about what you mean?"

"Okay, I mean first of all I like you guys," he started, "but I'm just not sure what we're doing here. We get together, talk, then read some chapter or watch a video and have some prayer requests. And again, that's fine. But is it just like we hang around each other, we talk about some Christian stuff, and then we just mature?"

"Huh," Stuart replied, thinking.

"Bottom line, I guess I just don't feel like anything's changing for me," Mike continued, sounding like he was just coming to this realization himself. "We made those goals at the beginning about growing together, and that sounded good, but it doesn't seem to be happening. Just speaking for me here."

"Huh," Stuart said again. "Mike, that's a great point."

Mike looked surprised, then shrugged. "Again, maybe it's just me. I don't know."

"No, I feel the same," Keisha said after a thoughtful moment. "I like you guys too, by the way," she added, getting a small chuckle from the group. "I feel great about the relationships, but our initial goals of maturing and growing in our faith—does that just happen if we do this long enough? And not to complicate it, but sometimes we just catch up and never get to the study and other times I wish we had more time to catch up. I'm not even sure which one I prefer."

Stuart and Leslie looked at each other, and then Stuart looked back at the group. "Well first, definitely fighting a moment of shame here because I feel like that is part of our role leading the group. I just wanted to share that I'm feeling a moment of 'oh crap' right now. Second, man, thanks for saying that, Mike. I hadn't even realized that we're kind of adrift, I guess. Honestly, I think I just assumed that if we were around each other and had some Scripture, it would just, well, *happen* if we gave it enough time." He shrugged at Leslie.

"Same here," she nodded, frowning in thought. "I think you're right on the money, Mike and Keisha." She looked at them. "But honestly, I have no clue what to do about it. Stuart, we should talk to Tim and Jane."

"Good call. And seriously, thanks," Stuart reiterated. "I have a feeling this is going to be really important for us. Let's touch back on this next week."

• • •

El Felix, Monday Night, 6:45 p.m.

"Honestly, the more I think about it, the more I think I just assumed that growing and maturing would somehow magically happen." Stuart shook his head in frustration. "Like if we knew and liked each other, and we studied something, then *voila!* We'd see all this transformation. But that's not happening. What gives?"

Tim and Jane nodded thoughtfully. Jane tipped her drink in Tim's direction, indicating that he should go first.

Tim cleared his throat. "First, let me say how proud I am of you both. Honestly admitting to your group that 'we don't know' is amazing, and it shows growth in *your* life. Do you remember when we met you here after your first meeting and you guys had just kind of faked your way through leading? From what you're telling us, last Thursday was the opposite. That's huge."

Stuart shrugged, a little uncomfortable with the compliment. "Thanks. I think."

Tim grinned and continued. "Second thought, you aren't as far off as you might think. We really are affected more than we know by who we spend time with, but the change is often subtle. Healthy relationships lead to growth, but it just takes time. You can't get what you are hoping for overnight. Okay, so my third thought just to keep them coming . . . let me ask you something, Stuart. What are your meetings at work like?"

Stuart laughed halfheartedly. "Depends who's running them! When Alice is in charge, they're awesome. Super focused and organized. I actually feel like there's a point. When George runs them—well, let's just say it's the opposite. I spend most of the meeting wondering why the heck I'm even there."

"Because you want it to be worth your time, right?" Tim prompted. "And you're saying when Alice runs meetings, she has a plan and a purpose. And what does George do or not do?"

"He just throws out a problem and hopes we'll get somewhere with it." Stuart paused. "Yeah, I see what you're getting at. But I don't want our group to feel like highly planned business meetings. It should be more organic and Spirit led, right?

Tim smiled, "I'd love to tell you that A plus B in a small group equals amazing relationships and spiritual growth, but I'd be lying. I tried that. Got a gold star and everything. It didn't work. That said, there are definitely groups that seem to move along this journey together with greater intentionality, and how they use their limited time together makes a big difference."

"Just like good leaders at work, good small group leaders understand the integral elements of a meeting that help the team accomplish what they hope for. You just have to find out which elements help you achieve your goals."

"Early on, we did the same thing," Jane added. "We just kind of hoped with the right ingredients, growth and maturity would take care of themselves. We figured as long as we were together for ninety minutes, the rest would just happen." Jane shrugged.

"Actually, your group is ahead of the curve. It takes most

groups about a year or two of meeting to hit the wall and wonder if they're missing something. Most groups usually just peter out or split up. At least that was my experience in the first couple groups I was a part of. We started trying different things and after a while we felt like we found a good structure that seemed to work consistently."

"Okay. Keep talking." Stuart motioned.

Jane laughed. "Well, we eventually figured out that people really needed to connect, to learn, and to live it out. Therefore, we structured our time around those three things."

Leslie leaned forward. "Connect, learn, live. Okay, that seems pretty simple. How do you balance them?"

"We'll get to that," Tim said. "But, first, I think it's important to understand these three parts of a group before trying to implement them. If you want to have an authentic group, and I know you do, then the connect piece is pretty obvious. When you connect relationally, you start building a foundation of trust. Then, as you begin to trust each other, you become more known and loved. All the other significant, transformational stuff is built on that foundation of trust—being known and experiencing love. One of the problems with a lot of groups is they become overly focused on content. They're there to study together, but they don't take the time to really connect."

"Ugh, we were in a group like that," Stuart nodded to Leslie. "We really liked the people in our group. The information we studied was practical and helpful, but I didn't feel like we were any closer after our eighteen months together. After the second or third week it was clear; we were in high school classroom mode. Sometimes you could tell the lesson really stirred something up in someone. But just as they'd start to open up about what was going on in their life, the facilitator would jump in and say, 'I'm so glad this brought that to mind.' Then they would just keep moving along."

"That's rough," Jane wrinkled her nose. "But I'm guessing you've been in groups that were kind of the opposite, too. Groups that 'hung out' a lot but didn't really learn much or grow together. You know, the supper club safe route."

"I'm afraid that's where our group is headed right now," Leslie said. "But yes, I was in a mom's group for a few months, and it was mostly just chit chat that sometimes drifted into gossip. We talked plenty, but rarely about anything of substance. I didn't feel *connected* in that group."

THE KEY TO CONNECTION IS FOUND IN ASKING QUESTIONS.

Jane nodded her head. "Connection is about more than conversation. You can have a nice conversation in the line at the grocery store. Real connection implies substance. As the leader, you have a chance to guide the conversation towards things that matter. This fosters real connection. The key to connection is found in asking questions."

Jane leaned forward, "Did you know that Jesus asks over three hundred questions in the gospels?[13] Jesus was an incredible question asker, and asking questions was a central part of his ministry."

Stuart gave a wry smile, "Man, that's your secret, Tim. I still remember when you asked me, 'Why do you trust yourself to provide for your family more than God?' That question wrecked me—in a good way. I still think about that."

Tim smiled. "Yep. That's a question every man needs to wrestle to the ground at least once in his lifetime. It's pretty crazy how a single question can make room for God to speak to you."

Jane jumped in. "Stuart, you think Tim just thinks up deep questions like that in the middle of a meeting? No way. You don't know about his question list?"

"Whoa now," Tim held up his hands, "Stuart still thinks I am a deep-thinking genius! Don't ruin his illusion. But I'm pretty sure Leslie's onto me, so I can tell her. I keep a list of good, open-ended questions on a document on my computer to use in the connect time of our groups."

"If you ain't cheatin', you ain't tryin'." Leslie winked and Tim laughed.

12 Questions

Use one of these twelve questions to facilitate the Connect time at the beginning of a small group meeting. They are in no specific order, and are developed to be a catalyst for deep connection around different aspects of life.

- In what area of life could you place more trust in God?

- How would your spouse or someone you are close to describe your relationship with them currently?

- What area of your life is not aligned with the direction you want to be heading?

- What are you currently passionate about?

- How is the healthier you five years from now different than the you of today?

- What is one thing about your spiritual life you'd like to see change in the next six months?

- In what way are you trying to seem better than you really are?

- Where is there potential for your character and integrity to be compromised?

- What is one thing you've done or experienced in the past sixty days that you're proud of?

- Where do you feel behind?

- What is your dominant emotion right now and why?

- What is something in the way of your spiritual or personal growth?

Leslie reviewed. "Okay, for the first connect part we have the opportunity to add intentionality to the social time with good questions. We spend some time there. Then what?"

Tim picked up, "Once you have some social or relational time, it's helpful to incorporate some content in your group to help guide the conversation. Read something out of the Bible, talk about a chapter of a book, bring in an article, watch a short video, or go through a small group curriculum. And don't feel like you always have to have a book or a study or some big production. You'd be amazed how impactful it can be to just read through some scripture as a group and discuss it."

"Okay, we've been doing these first two parts pretty well," Stuart shrugged at Leslie. "I mean we could be more intentional with good questions in our social connecting time at the beginning, but we've been making our way through Ephesians just by reading a chapter and then talking about it."

Tim held up a finger, "Well, that brings us to our third and most important part of any group—living it out. Truth is like paint. Lots of people go out and get some truth, like a can of paint from the home improvement store. Then they just let it sit on the shelf. They never do anything with it other than admire it on the shelf. They look at it and smile. 'It's so great that I have what I need to brighten up that room.' You have acquired the paint, but nothing's gonna change until you apply it. Applying the paint is where the real work comes in. To do it right can be tedious and very frustrating. It's messy. But it's the only way you're going to actually see that room change. In your group, growth—or applying the truth and living it out—should get the lion's share of your time, energy, and attention."

Leslie asked, "How do you shift gears from one to the other? I always felt like your group with you two was structured, but it never seemed rigid."

Jane smiled. "I'm so glad to hear that! That was our goal. We always have a loose structure in mind, but we leave room for flexibility. Roughly speaking, we like to give about 30% of our time to connecting, 20% to learning, and 50% to talking about how we're going to live it out or grow."

Stuart was surprised. "Wait, what? You devote only 20% of

your time to the actual material or curriculum? I'm confused then. What is the difference between learn and live? We watch something or read something and talk about it? That's learn and live, right?"

"Ahhh," Jane said, "you are onto the key to true growth. Don't miss this subtle but significant difference. See, most groups learn about something and then just talk about it. They feel better about themselves for feeling smarter, like they know a little more about God. But only truth that is trusted transforms. In other words, you've got to act on it. You've got to dig into how you're going to live it out."

Tim nodded, "But don't miss what we're really saying here. This isn't behavior modification, and it definitely isn't a checklist. We are talking about trusting God with our lives, which results in different actions and behavior change, not the other way around. There is a massive but subtle difference baked into what Jane just said that 'only truth that is trusted transforms.' She isn't saying

ONLY TRUTH THAT IS TRUSTED TRANSFORMS.

'truth trusted' means 'go do stuff.' She means that trusting truth *leads to* transformation or doing stuff. You see, most of us end up trying to *do* things and change our behavior in hopes that our heart will change as a consequence of our actions. We think that if we try hard enough, then we will finally be good enough for God. It's so easy to go there. It is just easier for us to strive to obey and try harder to do better because that keeps *us* in control. And a bonus is that we feel better about ourselves for trying harder. The problem is that it often leads us to feeling like exhausted failures. Not really the recipe for the peace Jesus alludes to, but most Christians don't know another way."

Leslie held up her hands. "Okay I don't want to miss this. I am not sure I know what the difference would look like in our group." Tim thought for a moment. "Put it this way. Say you're studying Ephesians where Paul says, 'be patient with one another.' You get to this application part of your group. And you, Stuart, recognize that you're not very patient with your kids. In wanting to obey, you commit to counting to three before responding to your kids. You give others permission to ask you about it. There you have it—living out the Scriptures. Not bad in itself, right? But look at the difference. You might faithfully count to three the next several weeks, and the group might ask you about it, and then you get a gold star for completing your commitment. But you totally miss unpacking the motive that led to the behavior in the first place. On the other hand, if you didn't follow through with your commitment, you would feel like a failure or be tempted to pose and lie about it. But has anything really changed? Maybe a tiny bit. But most likely you've just gritted it out and modified a behavior without addressing the heart issues. We aren't talking about behavior modification; we are talking about heart change."

> I TRIED FOR DECADES TO STRAIGHTEN UP, TO MEASURE UP. BUT I JUST ENDED UP TIRED AND WONDERING WHAT I WAS MISSING.

Jane was smiling at her husband's enthusiasm as Tim continued, "That's the power of the question, 'What faith step is God inviting me to take?' Because that question points to a different type of application. It's a type of application that takes trust, that has to do with our motives and our heart. Do you see how that is different than quickly jumping to "What should I do?""

I tried for decades to straighten up, to measure up. But I just ended up tired and wondering what I was missing. See, when I began to trust that I was a new creation, imparted with the very righteousness of Christ, I read the Bible differently. I saw obedience differently. I stopped striving as much and started trusting more. I began to trust God with areas of my life that seemed misaligned with my new identity as a son of God."

Three Key Questions

TO HELP SHIFT CONTENT DISCUSSION TO GROWTH AND LIFE APPLICATION

1. What does this mean for me personally?

2. What faith step is God inviting me to take?

3. How can we help each other?

Jane leaned in, "We obviously get excited about this and don't want to preach. It's a slow, day by day journey, but we get to start every day with an awareness of our need to trust God's grace, which will help us mature into who he says we are. And, over the years I have seen a massive shift in Tim's life and mine since we began to understand this grace of God more fully. As you both know, I have really struggled with fears of financial insecurity. I put so much pressure on Tim and myself to figure it out. But even as our margin grew, my anxiety about it didn't change. I would browbeat Tim about our budget. Then I finally asked myself *why* I was so anxious. It was because I believed our provision was up to us! Well, once I said it out loud, I knew that wasn't right. It was only after I began to trust God more deeply to take care of us that my anxiety and fears decreased. This grace thing is kind of counterintuitive. Trust in God used to feel and sound passive to me, but it's really the opposite. And it's really hard."

Tim continued without a beat, "So hard that we can't do it on our own. Our Father knew that, though, and gave us the Holy Spirit to help. We get to trust the Holy Spirit to help us trust God with these parts of our lives. *That* is the grace of God."

Stuart replied, "Being honest, I don't think I fully understand that yet."

Tim smiled, "Honestly, I don't either. Every day I wake up asking God to help me trust him more fully because every day I don't *want* to need God. I want to go back to doing it on my own. That position of humility and dependence is what leads to maturing, and we'll spend the rest of our lives figuring that out one day at a time. Shoot, if I could figure it out, I wouldn't need God to show up anymore, which would kind of mess the whole thing up anyways!"

Stuart set down his taco. "I think that might be the reason I feel so worn out as a Christian, like I'm always behind. I also think that's pretty different from most group discussions I've been a part of when we tend to just focus on application of what we learned without considering our motives."

Jane nodded, "Well said! The live it out section is the joy and fruit of living with Jesus. And remember, you two, these are just our suggestions for a general structure—no prescriptions or rigid format. Follow the Spirit where he leads. These are just principles that help our group time be more intentional and help us honor each other and achieve our goals.

Tim stretched back and put his hands behind his head, "Most of the time, the very best thing you can do as a leader is shut up and listen. Listen to them and listen to God. If you feel compelled to say something, then whenever possible, try to ask a question instead. A beautiful question can lead someone else to self-discovery. That's the magic. That's as good as it gets. And don't worry, you'll know when God moves in on your meeting. Just go with the flow."

IF YOU FEEL COMPELLED TO SAY SOMETHING, THEN WHENEVER POSSIBLE, TRY TO ASK A QUESTION INSTEAD.

Suddenly Tim leaned forward and laughed, "Well that wasn't exactly practicing what I was preaching, was it?" He shook his head. "I just talked at you two about the importance of asking questions instead of asking *you* questions! I probably could have gotten the point across a lot better that way. Call this one a miss but hey—I'm still working on this stuff, too!"

· · ·

What You Just Saw

Our time here on Earth is far more limited than we usually realize. When put in light of eternity, our lives are "a mist that appears for a little while and then vanishes."[14] When we get in

89

touch with this truth, we begin to see how valuable our time truly is. We must use our time on purpose and for our purpose, giving it to what matters most and limiting time spent on the unimportant. This is why the fourth Core Component is to *design your time for transformation.*

. . .

Why This Matters in Groups

If a ship is heading towards a destination, the captain and the crew need a vessel that's built for the journey. Your group meeting time is the ship that helps carry your group along this journey. Is the structure of your meeting time helping or hurting your group as you try to reach your destination?

As Tim and Jane showed us earlier, great groups embody intentionality and purpose. Typical groups function with little prior thought or plan in terms of how they spend their time together. Transformational groups use their time to intentionally pursue their purpose. They also evaluate their effectiveness regularly. Don't leave this up to chance or hope a good structure will create itself. There are lots of ways you can structure your time together as a group, and it should be built around what your group wants and needs. What is most important is that you have a plan.

TRANSFORMATIONAL GROUPS USE THEIR TIME TO INTENTIONALLY PURSUE THEIR PURPOSE.

After evaluating hundreds of groups to understand the most effective cadence for the group time, the best group structure I found was exactly what Tim was talking about: connect, learn, live. You need to spend time connecting relationally, or you short-circuit this whole process. You need to intentionally learn together, whether that's a curriculum, a scripture passage, TED Talk, or anything else that guides you into new understanding or awareness. And last, you've *got* to find ways for it to soak into your life. We shouldn't just connect and talk and then go back out and live the same as we did before.[15] If we want to grow, we need to start letting our time in our groups infiltrate our everyday lives.

You might be asking, "Okay, so how do we apply these truths in our lives without it feeling like we're 'fixing' or settling for sin management?" The answer lies in our foundation of how we view God and ourselves. Don't worry, if you are asking these questions you are on the right path!

IF WE ARE GROWING AND MATURING, WE WILL SEE A CHANGE IN HOW WE LOVE OTHERS.

Let's be clear. An authentic and grace-oriented group isn't something we just pay lip service to. It's not just a nice group in theory. If we are growing and maturing, we will see a change in how we love others.[16] Loving others is hard, but it is *because* we love each other that we are committed to following up with each other as we pursue living out the change we hope to see in our lives. This isn't keeping each other in line or becoming the behavior police. It's genuinely walking with each other. It's the difference between checking up on someone and checking in with someone.

If I'm struggling to prioritize time with God and bring that to my group as something I really want to put into practice in my life, then I sure hope they love me enough to follow up. That can look different depending on one's view of God, though. It could look like accountability based on "shoulds" and shame. However, in health, it looks like my brother pulling *for* me and pulling *with* me to help me grow into *who we both already know I am in Christ.* It's the difference in life-sucking "accountability" and life-giving sharpening. It may seem like semantics, but I promise the difference is literally life changing.

Last, don't overthink the structure. There will be times when you throw the whole plan out the window. Someone will walk in the door having just received terrible news or ready to confess something they've been hiding, and you'll know that leading the group to come around them is far more important than what you had prepared. Be intentional with your time but also be flexible and listen to the Spirit.

. . .

Practical Group Application

I suggest having an open conversation about this with your group. Ask questions like:

- How could we make better use of our time together?
- Is there a better meeting structure?
- Is there anything missing in our time together that we'd like to add?
- What ends up happening in our group that distracts us from our purpose?

We've included some good reflection questions in *Embark* to help your group members think this through. I know I keep driving it home, but the important thing here is to design your time *on purpose*, and that means prioritizing time to discuss this with your group.

Leader Resources

Use **Design Your Time** at *trueface.org/cureforgroups* to take notes for this discussion, and then record how you want to use your time on your **Group Map.**

Reflection Questions

1 In your personal life, how do you feel about how you're spending your time?

2 When you think of this model of connect, learn, and live, which aspect are you most drawn to? Why?

3 If you've been in a group before, how has the application aspect played out? Has it been glossed over? Used as a measuring stick? Something else?

№ 05

The Route

PLAN AHEAD TO GET WHERE YOU WANT TO GO

"Destiny is not fate, it's navigation."

—RICHIE NORTON

One of the most critical responsibilities in sailing is navigating the route. The navigator has all kinds of information at their disposal: depth, tidal patterns, local and global wind patterns, weather forecasts, wave heights, currents, and hazards. It's a constant process of zooming out to see the big picture and then zooming in to make sure all is well in your immediate vicinity on the vast ocean. You need to know the route you intend to take and then consistently check in to make sure your ship is in line.

There is a combination of flexibility and focus when it comes to navigating a ship. You need to know your destination, and you need to plot a route to get there. If you have an incredible, exotic destination in mind, you won't reach it by waking up every morning, going out on deck, and asking, "Where do we think we should head today?"

In the same manner, you need to choose a destination and plot a route with your group. Have you ever been in a group where every few weeks you're having the "what should we study next" conversation? It's often a standard feature of the typical group. This is like only looking at the two miles around your ship. It might keep you off of the rocks, but you have little chance of reaching any particular destination. Transformational groups plan their route ahead of time, keeping their eyes on the destination and adjusting the route along the way when unforeseen circumstances come along.

. . .

Stuart and Leslie's Patio, Thursday Night, 6:45 p.m.

"Gosh, I'm thankful it's nice enough to sit outside," Leslie said as everyone settled themselves on the patio.

"I can't wait to tear this thing out," Stuart eyed the concrete under their feet. "Pavers, right Mike?"

"Definitely," Mike agreed.

"If you can get it to happen, Mike, then you're my new best friend," Leslie sighed. "He's been talking about changing the patio for years."

"Oh, we'll get it done," Mike assured her.

Stuart clapped his hands together. "Well gang, this week is our strategy session week. We've talked about our goals, we've talked about our commitments and values, and we all still seem to like each other enough to keep meeting." This earned a little round of laughs around the circle. "I think it would be cool if we looked at the next three to four months to actually plan ahead on some stuff. We can get some hang time on the calendar and also think through content."

"Oh, I love this," Dwayne leaned forward. "My last group never planned ahead and every other week we spent a whole session talking about what we should study next. Drove me nuts."

Leslie chuckled, "I definitely get that. But before we look at the next few months, let's look back at those goals we created in our first meeting," Leslie said as she flipped through her notebook. "Our goals are: 'We want to have real relationships where we live life together and truly know and trust each other.' and 'We want to help each other grow in love for God, self, and others.'" She shut her notebook. "Like we talked about last week, we will try to incorporate some type of teaching or learning into each group time as a catalyst for our conversations and growth. So, what are some of your preferences when it comes to studies—if you have any?"

Amy surprisingly jumped in first. "No long videos! Sorry, but sitting in a room and watching a thirty-minute sermon is just too much for me."

Mike continued without a beat, "No thousand-page books. I mean, I do read, but just not that much."

Keisha laughed and raised her hand and said, "Glad you said it instead of me because same! Life feels so busy right now that I get overwhelmed if there's a ton of reading." She continued, "I also like variety. Sometimes we can read scripture, sometimes we can do a video small group study, or a book, or just unpack Sunday's message. I don't like doing the same kind of study month after month."

Stuart took notes, "That's good. What about topics? And does anybody have any studies or books that they would like to do as a group?"

Erik spoke up, "Recently I've been thinking a lot about how I don't think I see myself the way God sees me. Or maybe I don't see God the way He really is. I don't know, something's off in that arena for me—I always feel like I'm one mistake away from God giving up on me. And I know that's not how I should feel," he added quickly, "but I can't seem to shake it. I'd love to find something that talks about that."

"I love that, Erik," Stuart said, and he meant it. "That feels like something worth studying. Let's find a teaching or curriculum on that."

"I'd love to do something around anxiety," Melissa spoke up. She had been so quiet the last few meetings. "Or, maybe about peace. I just feel so wound up all the time, and I try to trust Jesus, but . . . well, I guess like Erik said. I can't seem to shake it."

They went around the circle like that for a while, looking at different studies, talking about what they wanted and needed. At one point Leslie reached over and grabbed Stuart's hand, and he squeezed it back, knowing they were thinking the same thing. Here they were, really talking about what they needed as a group, forging their own path according to what *they* wanted to do.

They ended up with a plan. They were going to go through Ephesians, do a four-week study that Eric was going to find on how we view God, and they were going to go through a book that Melissa suggested on the peace of God.

Stuart raised his eyebrows at Dwayne, "Dwayne, is that enough of a plan for you?"

Dwayne leaned back, "Absolutely. Honest, that really helps me relax to know what the next few months will look like."

Leslie took up the reins, "Okay, so our goal is 'We want to have real relationships where we live life together and truly know and trust each other.' Let's figure out how we can prioritize that."

Stuart leaned forward as everyone thought for a moment. He hesitated, then spoke, "One of our mentors once told me, 'The best way to understand someone's priorities is to look at their calendar.' It was like a knife to the chest at the time, honestly, but it's been huge for me. I said at the beginning of this group that I wanted it to be a priority—I wanted you guys to be a priority. And I meant that. So, I really think we should *actually* put things on the calendar. Like, tonight."

Erik nodded. "I'm on board. Things don't happen if you don't pick a date."

"Agreed," Dwayne's deep voice rumbled. "I've actually been thinking that it would be really great to have you all up to our family cabin. It's only an hour and a half north; we could do a weekend together."

> THE BEST WAY TO UNDERSTAND SOMEONE'S PRIORITIES IS TO LOOK AT THEIR CALENDAR.

"I *love* that idea," Leslie said emphatically. Jane and Tim had actually suggested that they do a weekend away, and Leslie had been looking for a way to bring it up. "When would work for everyone?"

They all pulled up their calendars on their phones, comparing dates and previous plans. They eventually settled on a weekend two months away.

"This will be really cool," Amy said as she set her phone down. "Thanks for inviting us, guys." Keisha and Dwayne nodded, smiling.

"Okay, now what about the rest of the time? What else do we want to do? Do a holiday party, a family park day, hit a movie, or do some serving together? Or, you know, all of the above?" Stuart felt like he was on a roll.

"Definitely not nixing the other options because they sound great too, but I know I want to figure out if we could serve somewhere together," Keisha jumped in. "I think serving together would help focus on something important as a group." Keisha shrugged. Amy offered up a few ideas of places she had volunteered at, and the group started looking for dates.

Route Planning Questions

- Is it time for an overnighter?
- Do you have a balance of learning mediums (books, scripture, small group studies, video based, sermon based)?
- Do you have a balance of topics?
- Do you have a serving focus?
- Do you have social and/or family time on the calendar?
- Do you have your next Route-Planning Session on the calendar?

Stuart felt a weight lifted off his shoulders. They actually had stuff on the calendar. A birthday party for Stuart and Leslie's three-year-old next month, a guy's night out, a girl's night out, and a goal for Amy to set up a service project for the group in three months.

The most exciting part to Stuart was that they put another "group check-in" or "route planning session" on the calendar in five months—a time to reevaluate goals, check in on how everybody is doing, and do the same process of thinking through the next season's calendar and content plan.

"This sorta feels like our group with Tim and Jane," Leslie whispered to Stuart. Stuart grinned back at her.

• • •

What You Just Saw

Planning ahead of time is just downright helpful. For a family vacation, product launch, home renovation, career change, and hundreds of other scenarios, thinking through and plotting a course of action helps you line up your priorities, organize your time, and increase the likelihood of your goals actually happening.

Another reason why planning ahead is so vital in any area of life is because it allows you to prioritize what's *truly* important. Your calendar reflects your priorities. Unfortunately, that doesn't reflect too well on some of us, does it? Often our daily responsibilities and work end up dominating our calendar and squeezing out important relational time. Although we know that God designed us to grow in the context of relationships, it can be all too easy to let our relationships take a back seat to tasks that feel more pressing.

That's why the fifth Core Component is to plan ahead in order to get where you want to go. Planning ahead helps protect your priorities, it saves you time and the headache of having to make decisions every few weeks, and it increases your chances of actually reaching your shared destination.

. . .

Why This Matters in Groups

Plotting the route and planning out a "semester" or "season" at a time will help you lead with a higher degree of intentionality and create deeper connections in your group. This not only makes things easier for you as the leader, but it helps your group engage for the long term. You don't want a cookie-cutter, plodding-along group. You want one that is specifically tailored for those of you actually *in* the group. Planning together helps you shape that reality.

PLAN AHEAD IN ORDER TO GET WHERE YOU WANT TO GO.

Exceptional leaders zoom out, look at the intended destination, and plot a course, taking into account things like margin, resources, and schedule. For those with kids, the month of May is usually pretty tricky. December is almost always crazy for everyone because of the holidays. Exceptional group leaders plan in advance to dial back the content during high volume months. They lean into more social time, or simple, one-off scripture studies that don't necessarily build from week to week. The point is to look and plan ahead.

When I was leading groups at North Point Community Church, I got to develop and oversee over fifty Leader Development Groups. These were nine-month leader trainings facilitated by pairs of the best leaders in the church. After we launched the first one, we constantly surveyed group members and leaders to see what was working and what wasn't. We would tinker and adjust different aspects of the group experience with a goal to yield better and better relational and spiritual outcomes for the group members. What emerged was a general superstructure for a group experience that resulted in significant growth—a map for the journey.

It's important to note that we didn't just start with a list of studies and activities and hope they got us to the X on the map. We started with the X on the map, dumped out the buckets, and carefully, prayerfully, chose the elements that we thought would get us there.

For those groups, we followed a journey that looked like:

- Build trusting relationships in the group.
- Focus on who scripture says God is (theology).
- Focus on how God sees us (identity).
- Explore priorities and relationships.
- Discover gifts and purpose.

Knowing your group's destination will help you plan ahead and evaluate what content or studies will best serve your group.

Most groups under plan. However, I want to make a disclaimer to be careful not to swing too far the other way. Keep your plans openhanded, and don't feel too married to your plan.

When we focus too much on content, we focus on sailing the boat without much regard for *where* we are sailing. When we develop a destination mindset, content and relational activities become the means to an end, not an end unto themselves.

Content and relational activities are the two primary parts of planning your route.

CONTENT

Content is what drives the learning part of your schedule. You can choose from some topical studies or you can build a structured schedule of curriculum that takes the group on a very specific journey. Depending on the group's maturity and interest level, amazing leaders prayerfully consider topics that are timely and aligned with the interests of the group.

CONTENT AND RELATIONAL ACTIVITIES ARE THE TWO PRIMARY PARTS OF PLANNING YOUR ROUTE.

In addition to intentionally picking the topic and sequence of your studies, know your group and their preferences. Content comes in all shapes, sizes, and qualities. You might love reading big, weighty tomes of truth, but you might lose some nonreaders if you don't ask about their preferences.

RELATIONAL ACTIVITIES

Relational time outside of your normal group meetings helps your group move beyond a book club and into that space of authentic community. There are lots of options like holiday parties, going to kids' sports games, service projects, and weekends away. The point is to experience your togetherness in a different arena than your regular meetings. These can be great for maintaining momentum through seasons when it will be more difficult to synchronize everyone's schedule. They are also great for bringing people back together after a time apart.

A survey we did revealed that an annual overnight retreat made one of the biggest differences in a group. The value of getting out of your element once a year in order to escape the busyness of life is one of the most important secret sauce components of transformational groups. Whatever you do, have fun! Have intentional conversation, sit on a dock, smoke a cigar. Just be together in another environment to make memories and spend quality time together. As David Ford reminds us, "Small groups that seek God's desires together have been at the heart of most of the major developments in the Church over the centuries. Whenever such a group breaks out of routine and has an intensive time together or with others, then transformation tends to happen."[17]

SERVING TOGETHER AS A GROUP ACCELERATES GROUP CONNECTION.

Serving together as a group accelerates group connection.[18] Serving together stretches us and creates shared memories and bonds while being the hands and feet of Jesus for others. With careful navigation, your group could discern and select an area or two outside of your group that could use your practical compassion. When we serve together, we naturally connect more deeply. As Coretta Scott King said, "The greatness of a community is most accurately measured by the compassionate actions of its members."

This sounds obvious, but relationships take time and intentionality. If you don't have one-on-one time with people in your group, time with each other's families, and time in social connection outside of the group, you won't experience the level of relationship that will transform your life.

• • •

Practical Group Application

There are limitless ways to practically plan your route and plot your course. Maybe you want to trade off who leads different studies or nominate one person to organize relational activities and service projects. Decide as a group what kind of route you want to plot. In *Embark*, the six-part study that pairs with this book, we provide lists of content topics, relational activities, and service areas to get you started. Give everyone some time to come up with answers to the three questions below for themselves.

At each Route-Planning Session, follow these five steps:

1. Begin by discussing these three questions as a group (we will unpack these more in the last section, *Tying Off*):
   • Are we maturing and continuing to grow?
   • Are we becoming more known by each other?
   • Are we overflowing and becoming more focused on others?

2. Revisit these parts of your group:

 Destination: Is our destination still correct? Do we need to shift it?

Captain: Are we being vulnerable with each other and growing in trust?

Crew: Are we reflecting our values and living by our commitments?

Ship: How are we spending our time together? Does anything need to shift?

3. Give everyone a few minutes to ponder the following three questions, then share your answers.

- *How do I want to grow?* Maybe patience has really been on your mind. Perhaps a group member has never read much of the Old Testament and would like to get more familiar. Maybe you're a young married group, and some of you would love to dig into parenting and family dynamics.

- *How do I want to have fun with my group?* Laughing together and eating together are two incredible ways to build genuine connections. Do you love hiking? Is there a band coming to town you'd like to see together? Does someone want to host a beginning of summer pool party? Dream about ways to enjoy time together.

- *Where do I want to serve?* Is there a specific population or pain point that you feel connected to? Is there an area where you've been wanting to serve and would like to invite the rest of your group to join? Is there a need that could be met by several of you coming together? Paula Fuller highlights this profound outcome of serving together, "We are formed *in* mission, not merely *for* mission. As the good news of the gospel flows through us, we are changed from the inside out."[19]

4. **Start looking for similarities in everyone's answers.** Print out calendars from *trueface.org/cureforgroups* and start actually putting things on your calendar. Remember, your calendar reflects your priorities, so if you haven't written it down, odds are it won't happen.

5. **Don't miss this! Put another Route-Planning Session on the calendar.** This is a time to reevaluate goals, check in on how everybody is doing, and go through the same process of thinking through the next season's calendar and content plan.

One of the simplest, most effective things we observed in transformational groups was that they were very intentional to reset semester-based plans in January, May, and August—and yes, this means they put those meetings on their calendar too. You will do this same exercise at each of these meetings, planning out the next few months and putting a new route with relational activities and content on your calendar.

These rhythms for groups naturally follow the patterns of our lives, and they are the perfect time to plan out the curriculum and activities for the next four to five months. Prioritizing this time with your group will alleviate anxiety as a small group leader and will help you lead with a high level of intentionality.

Leader Resources

Use the **Route Planner** at *trueface.org/cureforgroups* as a guide for this discussion, and then record your upcoming content, relational activities, and service opportunities on your **Group Map.** Congratulations, your Group Map is now complete! Make sure to keep it—you'll want to reference is throughout your time. You'll especially want it at your next Route-Planning Session.

Reflection Questions

1 When you consider content, relational activities, and service, which feels the most difficult for you to prioritize? Why?

2 Based on your temperament and wiring, are these Route-Planning Sessions going to be easy or difficult for you?

3 How do you think this Route-Planning Session would have affected groups you have been in previously?

Tying Off

"A ship in harbor is safe, but that is not what ships are built for."

—JOHN A. SHEDD

Well done!

You've determined your destination as a group and chosen collective goals with a direction. This will help your group know why they're showing up, which will help them trust that it's worth their time.

You've dug into your role as the captain and explored why vulnerability is the foundational element of leading a transformational group. By spending the time to better understand how you see God and how you see yourself, you can give the incredible gift of authenticity and humility to your group.

You've developed a crew culture with values and commitments, choosing to intentionally create a safe, healthy environment. This will pay dividends when conflicts inevitably arise, and these values will give you a framework for addressing it together.

You've crafted a vessel to get you where you want to go, designing your time in your meetings on purpose and for your purpose. Our time here on Earth is precious, and by consciously choosing how you spend your time together you will honor your group's goals and time.

Lastly, you've plotted out a route to help get you where you want to go. Planning months at a time not only saves the entire group time and energy, it ensures you're moving toward your relational and spiritual goals.

So now what? Keep going!

Reevaluate as you go. Continue to model vulnerability. Keep your values and commitments in mind, and correct your course when you feel yourself or the group veering away from them. You're equipped to steer this ship wherever you and your group decide you want it to go, and the Spirit will help you determine where that is.

So, before we tie off, there are a few questions I want to address.

1. How will you decide if you should break up or wrap up your group, either individually or as a whole?

2. Why do we face choppy waters if we lead well?

3. What are simple things great leaders do as they navigate the journey?

Are We Breaking up?

Whether your group is just starting or whether you're in the middle of your journey and looking for a course correction, most groups will eventually come to an end. While some groups become lifelong groups, most undergo changes when people leave or the group disbands.

Should you leave the group? Should the group break up? When should it end? How can you conclude your group in a healthy way? Did you stay too long or give up too quickly? These are all important, highly relational questions. Asking the right question is critical for group leadership.

These are natural and good questions, but they aren't the best questions. There are three questions that help leaders and groups determine the best way forward. These questions are invaluable to you as the captain of the group. They will serve as a compass to help you determine your bearings. It is best if these are routinely asked at the Route-Planning Session before each season of a group.

ARE WE MATURING AND CONTINUING TO GROW?

The first question is, "Are we maturing and continuing to grow?" It's remarkably easy to drift into just learning information and skip the whole living it out part. Remember, spiritual maturity and spiritual growth are exemplified in our love for God, ourselves, and others. That happens when we trust and apply what we are learning in the context of those relationships.

ARE WE BECOMING MORE KNOWN BY EACH OTHER?

Is your time as a group helping produce that fruit in your life and the lives of the other group members? Are people in your life noticing a difference in how you love them? If the answer to these questions is "no," then reevaluate what kind of ship you're sailing, which is how you're spending your time together. Are you practicing that messy, spark-filled, iron sharpening iron aspect of healthy relationships? Are you digging into how you can apply truth to your real, daily lives?

The second question is, "Are we becoming more known by each other?" As we just talked about, having level three relationships is hard work. And as such, it's easy to get gridlocked at level two. Heck, it's easy to go *back* to level two when things get sticky. If the answer to this question is "no," it may be a good time to reexamine how you as the captain are modeling vulnerability and your crew culture, as well as your group's values and commitments. Where are you getting stuck or comfortable in the group? Is there a pattern emerging that dissuades people from sharing?

Third and last, "Are we becoming more focused on others?" God has designed each of us uniquely as parts of the Body of Christ. If we are continuing to mature and grow, then we will inevitably become more focused on others. We will begin using more of our time, talents, and treasures to love and serve others, rather than focusing solely on our own needs. If the answer to this question is "no," then you may need to replot your route or go back to the drawing board and design a new and better ship. Do you need to include more service opportunities? Would it help to set aside time to encourage each other to be bolder in trusting God with how you use your time, talents, and treasures for the benefit of others? As we mature, it should show in how we love others.[20]

ARE WE BECOMING MORE FOCUSED ON OTHERS?

If the answer to these three questions is "yes," then keep on going! If the answer is "no," to any or all of the questions, then evaluate why that is. You may need to reevaluate your goals as a group or revise your route and activities. It might be time to form different groups. Perhaps some of you are feeling called to start neighborhood-specific groups to love those living in your proximity, or others of you may feel like you could be more vulnerable with and known by people in their own life-stage (parents of preschoolers, empty nesters, etc.). That's okay. Asking and honestly answering those three questions will help you evaluate where you want to go next, both individually and collectively.

. . .

Why Should You Expect Choppy Waters?

Real groups deal with real stuff. Some groups stay at a depth that avoids choppy waters, and they miss out on a life-changing opportunity to grow and heal. Lack of choppy waters isn't always a good thing. It could indicate that you are staying in shallow waters relationally in order to avoid the deeper wounds that live with each of us.

Because most of our wounds have a relational component, our healing needs to have a relational component too. That is why

SOME GROUPS STAY AT A DEPTH THAT AVOIDS CHOPPY WATERS, AND THEY MISS OUT ON A LIFE-CHANGING OPPORTUNITY TO GROW AND HEAL.

groups can serve as a safe environment for men and women to experience healing, which inevitably leads to life change. And while this life change is a beautiful thing, it's never *easy*. I wish I could tell you how to make change easier, but I can't.

Change is something you have to go *through*, and it's difficult. Most of our wounds and hurts change our experience of God's

THE CURE FOR GROUPS

love, how we view ourselves, and how we engage with others. At some point in your group, people are going to get hurt. It may be in their personal lives or between group members. It may be the pain of old wounds that are being inflamed again. All of us are wounded and broken in various ways.

Where there are relational wounds and hurts, shame is usually right there alongside the wound. Shame hisses lies, leading to disunity and confusion. Shame affects how we think about God and ourselves, significantly impacting our relationships with others. That is why shame keeps us from moving from level two friendships to level three, deep friendships. In order to move into these authentic, intentional relationships, we must continue to believe that Jesus has taken care of our shame. We must continue to trust him and others, even when we feel fear and shame rising up in us. This is difficult, sacred work. Don't be surprised when you face these waters as a group. Instead, look for the opportunity to replace those lies with truth and venture into the deep waters of truth *together*.

One reason Jesus intended your group to set sail as a loving community is that love heals. Most people have lived most or all of their lives without the benefit of a loving community. They have learned to cope through the failed but familiar placebos of self-help and sin management, all the while needing only to trust the love of God and others to experience healing. Authors Henry Cloud and John Townsend cite the gnarly symptoms of a life without trusted community—neediness, passivity, aggressiveness, condescension, overbearingness, withdrawal, arrogance, talking too much, and more.[21] When we trust others, we allow them to know our weaknesses and help us mature. This simply does not happen without deeper connection. Most of us have found it difficult to heal these unruly areas because we are either missing safe groups or lacking trust in others—or both.[22]

You have the opportunity to create a transformational group that leads to deep relationships and spiritual growth that you will remember for the rest of your lives. That is a sacred and amazing opportunity. Seize it and enjoy it. You will fail at times. Keep going. Your group will hit choppy waters. Keep going. These are just opportunities to trust in the abundant grace of God to sustain us through the Holy Spirit.

• • •

Keep It Simple

Don't be overwhelmed by the role or the opportunity. You were made for this. While it is incredibly significant, it is also simple. Jesus modeled a relational ministry that we can emulate. I have experienced and watched discipleship and transformation happen in groups. When it does, these three components are a part of the life-changing relationships.

First: **Be consistent.** It's hard to build trust and be known by someone without consistent time together. That's why most of our friends came from school, work, or church, because consistency is built into those relationships. We see and spend time with them regularly. Without consistency, relational time gets squeezed into the nonexistent margins of our weeks. In other words, it doesn't happen. Consistency is loving because it meets our relational needs of feeling safe and supported. Love others by being consistent.

Second: **Be intentional.** Authentic relationships don't happen with consistency alone. There are plenty of people we consistently spend time with but don't have deep friendships with (like your coworkers, classmates, golf buddies, or the lady that always sits behind you at church). We can even have weekly lunches with a friend but keep it surface level. Instead, when we're intentional with our relationships, we are willing to risk vulnerability, challenge each other, and pursue emotional connections. We aren't just spending time together because there's nothing good on TV. We know our time together counts, and we treat it that way.

Finally: **Ask the second question.** "How's that project at work?" "Did you end up calling your mom last week?" or even, "How are you doing?" are all great first questions. However, the real power is in the second question, the one that leans into how they answer the first. A good second question is penetrating and draws out a more thoughtful or emotional response. For example, you might ask a friend, "How are your kids doing with the move?" They might reply, "They're doing okay." Our tendency is to move on to the next topic, but the power is when we stop, listen, and then ask the second question. This might look like, "What's been the hardest part?" or "Who seems to be struggling the most?" The art of asking good follow-up questions is a skill every single one of us can grow in, and since conversations are the primary vehicle for relational connection, honing this skill will pay dividends. If you're trying to get to know someone or connect on a more authentic level, then ask the second question.

In reality, these three pieces are our imperfect, human effort to model how Jesus acted in relationships. Jesus himself carried these out perfectly. He didn't run into Peter when it was convenient or catch up with John every six months. He consistently spent time with them, day in and day out. He was also deeply intentional, fully present in his interactions and conversations, knowing that each word he spoke mattered greatly. And lastly, he asked thought-provoking questions to connect with people, to draw them out and make them think deeply about their own lives and hearts. When this process of developing level three, deep relationships gets hard—and it will—trust the process. Be consistent, be intentional, and ask the second question.

. . .

Bon Voyage!

God designed us to live in real, authentic relationships. It's how we grow and mature, and it's also one of the primary ways God infuses joy and meaning and *life* into us. So, dive in! Your small group doesn't have to suck. Don't settle for mediocre relationships and boring groups. Hoist the sails, throw off the bowlines, and yeah, you know, all that stuff. Be brave, trust God's Spirit, and set sail into the wild waters of life-giving groups. You won't regret it.

> *"Twenty years from now you will be more disappointed by the things you didn't do than by the ones you did do. So throw off the bowlines! Sail away from safe harbor. Catch the trade winds in your sails. Explore. Dream. Discover!"*

—MARK TWAIN

Acknowledgments

This book is the by-product of a lot of shared wisdom. It is the fruit of a team of people helping me.

Most all of what I know has been modeled and shared with me by multiple men and women who have served as mentors on this journey of following Jesus. Emily, your amazing wisdom and maturity has had the greatest impact on my life. Moses, Zane, Naomi, Jude, Titus, Valor, Emmie, and Eli, I couldn't be prouder to be your dad. Kids, I pray that you experience relationships where you are fully known and fully loved. I pray that you experience the types of relationships that Jesus makes possible with God, yourselves, and others. I hope you always trust our loving and good Father. Mom and Dad, Robert Bruce Angle, Jr. and Emily (yes my mom and wife have the same name just like me and my dad), thank you. You have been a model of faithfulness and trust in God throughout my life.

The sacrificial investment that people have made in me has been a key part in developing me into the man I am today. Clay Walkup, Drew Anderson, and Bo Lancaster, you were my first group. Ray Strickland, you took me under your wing in high school and modeled intentionality at a young age. Herbert Wagemaker, you bought me Steamers for lunch almost every week at UF. Benj Miller and Scott Bowen, thanks for modeling level three relationships. You are stuck with me for life. Stuart and Leslie, Blake and Megan, David and Keisha, Jason and Marie, thanks for being my current group, and I hope we talk about it the rest of our lives. Scott and Stormy Morrison, thanks for believing in me, investing in me, and guiding me in this season. I am excited for partnering in ministry in the years ahead. Tim and Anne Baker, your passion and support has inspired me. Dennis and Jane, you have and will continue to lead me as a wise guide. Last, Regi and Miriam Campbell, I want to be like you when I grow up. I miss you like crazy, Regi.

My time at North Point was the testing ground for this passion God has put on my heart. Lee Rogers, you were my right-hand man (or was I yours?) the whole time. Clay Scroggins, you are the best boss I've ever worked for. You are an incredible friend and co-leader and pastor. David Ingmire, Jason Day, John Swails, Dennis Worden, Justin Elam, Clint Nowery, Bill Willits, Andy Stanley, and all of the LDG mentors who experimented with me . . . it was fun getting into trouble with you for the Kingdom.

John Lynch, Bill Thrall, and Bruce McNicol, thanks for being mentors over the years. Your faithfulness over twenty-five years of Trueface has impacted hundreds of thousands, including me. Thanks for entrusting and empowering me to carry the baton. Thanks for exemplifying humble leadership in letting me do that. Bruce, your input and support of me in writing this book was a game changer.

This book was made possible with the help of a team. Brittany Sawrey, you carried most of the load and made this project happen. You are an incredible writer, project manager, team member, and wise Jesus follower. Jonny and Abby Wills, Chris Arias, and John Blase, we couldn't have done it without your writing genius. Pat Malone, you made our vision for this book come alive through design. To the draft readers that helped us make it better, thanks.

And finally, to the Trueface staff team, I love being on this adventure with you. To my amazing board, Scott Morrison, CE Crouse, Steen Hudson, Lindy Black, Delphine Fanfon, Dennis Latimer, and Pete Loescher, thanks for your leadership. Thank you to all the faithful donors who have given throughout the years to Trueface in order to help this ministry help people experience the peace and freedom of the original good news. Let's continue to equip people to understand who God says they are and experience authentic community.

Endnotes

1. David Kinnaman and Mark Matlock, *Faith for Exiles: 5 Ways for a New Generation to Follow Jesus in a Digital Babylon* (Grand Rapids: Baker, 2019), 113.
2. 1 John 4:18.
3. John Lynch, Bruce McNicol, and Bill Thrall, *The Cure: What If God Isn't Who You Think He Is and Neither Are You* (Dawnsonville, GA: Trueface, third edition, 2016).
4. 2 Corinthians 5:21; Romans 8:15.
5. Genesis 1:27.
6. Genesis 18:14, 21:2; Isaiah 55:11; Mark 1:15; Ephesians 1:10; Psalm 90:12, 119:105; Proverbs 11:14, 16:3; Luke 14:28–33; James 4:13–15.
7. John Lynch, Bruce McNicol, and Bill Thrall, *The Cure: What If God Isn't Who You Think He Is and Neither Are You* (Dawnsonville, GA: Trueface, third edition, 2016), 77.
8. 2 Corinthians 5:17; Galatians 6:15; Ephesians 4:24.
9. Romans 1:7; 1 Corinthians 1:2; Ephesians 2:19; Colossians 1:12.
10. Pete Scazzero, *The Emotionally Healthy Church* (Grand Rapids: Zondervan, 2003), 122.
11. If you'd like to do a deeper dive in understanding our view of God and ourselves, our team unpacks that to a greater degree in the book *The Cure*.
12. Ruth Haley-Barton, *Strengthening the Soul of Your Leadership* (Grand Downers Grove, IL: Inter Varsity Press, 2008), 127.
13. Martin B. Copenhaver, *Jesus Is the Question: The 307 Questions Jesus Asked and the 3 He Answered* (Nashville: Abingdon Press, 2014).

14. James 4:14.
15. James 1:22–25.
16. John 13:34–35.
17. David Ford, *The Shape of Living: Spiritual Directions for Everyday Life* (New York City: Harper Collins, 1997), 92.
18. Matthew 10:45.
19. Paula Fuller, *The Kingdom Life: Participating in God's Mission* (Colorado Springs: Navpress, 2010), 218.
20. John 13: 35.
21. Henry Cloud and John Townsend, *Making Small Groups Work: What Every Small Group Leader Needs to Know* (Grand Rapids: Zondervan, 2003).
22. For more on how this process works, see the Trueface book, Bill Thrall, Bruce McNicol, and Ken McElrath, *The Ascent of a Leader* (Dawsonville: Trueface, 1999), 81–89.

Ready to live this out in your group?

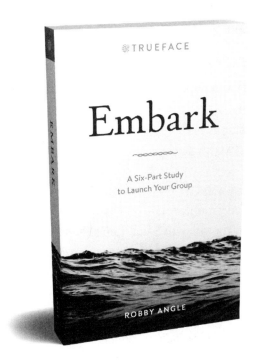

Through videos, group exercises and reflection questions, *Embark* will guide your group through the five Core Components, setting the foundation for a group you'll talk about the rest of your lives.

Visit ***trueface.org/embark*** to get your copies.

Robby Angle

Robby is the President and CEO of Trueface. He lives in Dawsonville, Georgia with his wife Emily and their eight children.

Prior to serving at Trueface, Robby served for over seven years at North Point Community Church in Atlanta, Georgia founded by Andy Stanley. In his role, Robby utilized Trueface resources through his positions as Director of Adult Ministry Environments and Director of Men's Groups.

Robby and Emily both worked as Licensed Professional Counselors, facilitating group therapy. Prior to joining North Point, they also served with Samaritan's Purse in Pakistan and Myanmar overseeing international disaster response teams. Robby and Emily received a Masters in Community Counseling from Appalachian State University. Angle also holds a business degree from the University of Florida, and a Certificate in Biblical studies from Dallas Theological Seminary.

He loves Trueface and the way it has created such a unique and effective way for teaching complex biblical principles of truth and grace and moving people from pleasing God to trusting God with their new identity.

TRUEFACE

beyond the mask

Today's culture is perfecting the art and science of creating masks. Behind these masks, people are dying inside. **We're here to change that.**

Trueface equips people to experience the freedom of living beyond the mask, because behind the mask is the real you. When we increase trust in our relationships, we are able to experience being more authentically known and loved by God and others.

We hope to be a bridge for hundreds of thousands to experience the peace and freedom of the original good news by trusting God and others with their whole selves . . . the self behind the mask.

To learn more about Trueface, visit trueface.org, or join the thousands of people living the Trueface life on social media.

Instagram: ***@truefacelife***

Facebook: ***@truefacecommunity***

Twitter: ***@truefaced***

Trueface is a non-profit supported by people who have been impacted by the ministry. To partner with us in creating resources, visit ***trueface.org/give.***

ℝ TRUEFACE

Small Group Studies

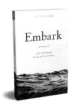

EMBARK

Our resource for starting a transformational small group, *Embark* is the companion group guide to *The Cure for Groups*. Through videos, discussion questions, and practical group applications, it guides you in creating a small group that's bursting with life, depth, and the kind of authentic community Jesus created us for.

TWO ROADS

Explore the first three chapters of *The Cure* in-depth with this small group study. *Embark* is designed to help your group travel beyond the mask and start experiencing real, authentic relationships through videos, discussion questions, scripture and application.

THE HEART OF MAN PARTICIPANT GUIDE

With contributions from Jackie Hill Perry, Dan Allender, WM Paul Young, Jay Stringer and John and Stasi Eldredge, this Trueface resource guides your group through unpacking and processing *The Heart of Man* movie and how to experience the love of the Father in the midst of our darkest struggles.

Books

THE CURE

Unpacking our view of ourselves and our view of God, The Cure invites you to remove your mask and experience God's lavish grace. This flagship book explores identity, community, sin, healing, destiny, and more as you discover that maybe God isn't who you think he is...and neither are you.

THE CURE AND PARENTS

Travel with the Clawson family on their summer vacation as they struggle to navigate their family dynamics. Told partly through narrative and partly through teaching, this resource is for anyone wanting to bring grace to their family.

BO'S CAFÉ

Steven Kerner is living the dream in southern California, until his wife kicks him out after another angry outburst. Walk with Steven and his eccentric mentor Andy as they explore Steven's unresolved problems and performance-based life, rediscovering the restoration and healing only God's grace can provide.

TRUST FOR TODAY

This 365-day devotional invites you to experience grace in your daily life, both in the big moments and the details of life. Use these short readings to incorporate grace into your everyday.

THE ASCENT OF A LEADER

Become the leader people want to follow by opening yourself up to the influences that develop character: enduring relationships with friends, family and God. *The Ascent of a Leader* guides you through cultivating extraordinary character in your home, company, community, and every other arena of life.

BEHIND THE MASK

When sin enters our lives, we have automatic, God-given responses. If we are the one who sinned, our response is guilt. If we are sinned against, our response is hurt. Explore these two involuntary responses and how they can lead to painful patterns of hiding and hurting, unless we allow the grace of Jesus to heal us.